Communicating in Professions and Organizations

Series Editor
Jonathan Crichton
University of South Australia
Adelaide, SA, Australia

This ground-breaking series is edited by Jonathan Crichton, Senior Lecturer in Applied Linguistics at the University of South Australia. It provides a venue for research on issues of language and communication that matter to professionals, their clients and stakeholders. Books in the series explore the relevance and real world impact of communication research in professional practice and forge reciprocal links between researchers in applied linguistics/ discourse analysis and practitioners from numerous professions, including healthcare, education, business and trade, law, media, science and technology.

Central to this agenda, the series responds to contemporary challenges to professional practice that are bringing issues of language and communication to the fore. These include:

- The growing importance of communication as a form of professional expertise that needs to be made visible and developed as a resource for the professionals
- Political, economic, technological and social changes that are transforming communicative practices in professions and organisations
- Increasing mobility and diversity (geographical, technological, cultural, linguistic) of organisations, professionals and clients

Books in the series combine up to date overviews of issues of language and communication relevant to the particular professional domain with original research that addresses these issues at relevant sites. The authors also explore the practical implications of this research for the professions/ organisations in question.

We are actively commissioning projects for this series and welcome proposals from authors whose experience combines linguistic and professional expertise, from those who have long-standing knowledge of the professional and organisational settings in which their books are located and joint editing/authorship by language researchers and professional practitioners.

The series is designed for both academic and professional readers, for scholars and students in Applied Linguistics, Communication Studies and related fields, and for members of the professions and organisations whose practice is the focus of the series.

More information about this series at
http://www.palgrave.com/gp/series/14904

Johanna Woydack

Linguistic Ethnography of a Multilingual Call Center

London Calling

palgrave
macmillan

Johanna Woydack
Foreign Language Business Communication
Vienna University of Economics and Business
Vienna, Austria

Communicating in Professions and Organizations
ISBN 978-3-319-93322-1   ISBN 978-3-319-93323-8   (eBook)
https://doi.org/10.1007/978-3-319-93323-8

Library of Congress Control Number: 2018956290

This Palgrave Macmillan imprint is published by the registered company Springer Nature Switzerland AG
The registered company address is: Gewerbestrasse 11, 6330 Cham, Switzerland

Praise for *Linguistic Ethnography of a Multilingual Call Center*

"Woydack provides an illuminating insider look into call centers and how call agents operate interactionally and textually, within the organization itself and with clients on the end of the phone line. The importance of the standardized script, which is frustratingly familiar to most people, is investigated in terms of top-down accountability, training, and monitoring alongside bottom-up resistance and agency on the part of call center agents. A fascinating ethnographic study of a multilingual globalized workplace."

—Colleen Cotter, *Queen Mary University of London, UK*

"This innovative study of a multilingual centre draws on unprecedented ethnographic access. Four years of participant observation provide Woydack with an insider understanding that enables her to challenge established critiques of standardization. Detailed analysis shows the agency of staff as they negotiate the demands of the script, their own communicative repertoires, and immediate interactional realities. Her research provides a fascinating glimpse into a little-understood setting, and a nuanced understanding of the contemporary workplace."

—Karin Tusting, *Lancaster University, UK*

"By placing script trajectories in the centre of this linguistic ethnography, Woydack constructs an insightful and engaging account of language practices in a globally operating call center. Her study weaves together recontextualization analysis and elements of workplace studies in a highly innovative way."

—Jannis Androutsopoulos, *University of Hamburg, Germany*

"This book provides a fresh and insightful exploration into how call centre agents develop and use language at work. The researcher was able to do this because of her unique position within this workplace: she being one of the agents herself. This allowed her to provide a deep ethnographic account of how agents are recruited, trained and managed in this call centre, where many previous studies have relied on less knowledge and understanding of the actual and nuanced work situation."

—Jane Lockwood, *The Hong Kong Polytechnic University*

Acknowledgments

I would like to extend my gratitude to several people who have contributed in various ways to this book.

I am greatly indebted to my Ph.D. supervisors Prof. Ben Rampton, Prof. Celia Roberts and Prof. Jannis Androutsopoulos, who have assisted me over the years. My warmest and deepest thanks go to my main supervisor Prof. Ben Rampton. I am sincerely grateful for all his extraordinarily helpful, meticulous and detailed comments on the various drafts, for being patient with me, taking time for supervision meetings and inspiring me to think deeper and differently about aspects of my work.

I am grateful to the Funds for Women Graduates (FfWG) for helping me with the funding of this research.

This book would not have been possible if it had not been for the management of my field site who kindly granted me full access and supported me the whole way through, always trying to facilitate my research. I do not know how to thank them enough for this. The same is true of all my participants, to whom I owe the greatest obligation for sharing their invaluable insights and knowledge and allowing me to represent their experiences in this book. It is their voices which have contributed greatly to its insights.

Last but not least, I would like to thank my family, in particular my parents, for their continuous support, help, and advice, since without this,

I would not have been able to complete this book. I am also very grateful to my brother for assisting me with the editing of this work and my sister and brother-in-law Geoffrey for helping me with the proofreading of some parts of it.

I gratefully acknowledge permission from Multilingual Matters for allowing me to reuse content from a chapter I published in the volume "Engaging in Superdiversity: Recombining Spaces, Times and Language Practices" and Cambridge University Press to draw on material from within: Woydack, J., & Rampton, B. (2016). Text trajectories in a multilingual call centre: The linguistic ethnography of a calling script. *Language in Society,* 45(5), 709–732 © Cambridge University Press 2016, reproduced with permission.

Contents

List of Figures

List of Tables

1

Introduction

As employees, most of us have probably received written instructions and guidelines from our colleagues or superiors that we were supposed to follow, carry out, or reference in workplace tasks (Smith 2001; Anderson 2004). Sometimes we adhere to these directives to the letter, or even find them helpful. At other times we might interpret them situationally or try to evade or even resist them. Creating a work culture encouraging employees' compliance with electronic or paper texts, also called "audit culture," "audit society," or "standardization," is on the rise (Strathern 2000; Power 2010; Shore and Wright 2015).

This book is about call center workplaces that have reputations in the public and the media for providing scripted "instructions" and guidelines to employees. The general public believes management uses electronic monitoring to insure that call center workers ("agents") follow these scripts (cf. Bain and Taylor 2000, 3; Hudson 2011). In many industries and institutions, providing employees with instructional texts is considered unproblematic, a positive aspect of the work environment oriented toward achieving and maintaining standards. However, scholars researching the dynamics of call center labor in which scripted directives govern work argue that the process is controversial and mostly negative. Sociologists and sociolinguists blame the scripted work environments of call centers for deskilling, dehumanization,

© The Author(s) 2019

J. Woydack, *Linguistic Ethnography of a Multilingual Call Center:
London Calling*, Communicating in Professions and Organizations,
https://doi.org/10.1007/978-3-319-93323-8_1

and the compromise of employee agency (cf. e.g., Mirchandani 2004, 359–62; Sonntag 2009, 12). In fact, these scholars often believe scripted work environments are so controlling and oppressive that workers find themselves driven to resist all forms of control; scholarship celebrates them for this (Mumby 2005; Bain and Taylor 2000; Leidner 1993) Many researchers believe that the agency inherent in humanity resists standardization attempts that turn workers into machines. If agents do support standardization, scholars argue in a Marxian fashion, they do not realize that they have been duped and exploited by the system (see also Mumby 2005). Yet the same researchers assume that agents are limited in their ability to resist because they work in an electronic prison where every keystroke is being recorded and work contracts are temporary, which means agents can lose their employment if they resist.

While I was working and doing fieldwork in call centers that relied heavily on scripts and monitoring, I was surprised to learn how supportive call agents themselves were of scripts. I did not expect agents to tell me that scripts, for example, helped them master languages or strengthen their fluency. This support stood in stark contrast to most of the academic literature and what one reads in the media (see for an exception Sallaz 2015). I asked myself if these workers were indeed being duped as the literature claimed, and if the only way for agents to show agency was to resist openly. Is it possible that other forms of agency, with some degree of compliance, could have been overlooked by researchers, such as the creative transformation of scripts in the practice of call center work itself?

I was also surprised by the different purposes for scripts at call centers and the diversity in perceptions of their utility. Corporate management thought of scripts and their uses in ways markedly different from the call center agents and the managers below them. Call center managers were varied amongst themselves in the positions they took toward scripts. Individuals adopted stances depending on when they were talking and to whom. Occasionally contradictions among workers surfaced in the form of open conflict. Yet scripts were also the thread that connected call center workers across the organizational hierarchy. A closer look at the functions of scripts and their efficacy in the workplace will help develop a more nuanced understanding of the controversies surrounding call center labor, and it will address the productivity of agents operating in these settings. The following vignette from my field notes illustrates some of the tensions and productive agentive strategies that will be the focus of this book.

Field Note Entry 1.1 Problems with a campaign and Jenny's secret solution

[I had received a Yahoo Instant Message from Jenny asking me to come to the panic room for an emergency meeting. I had already received a visit from the operations manager from upstairs asking me to fix a particular campaign where the numbers were very bad. As I walked into the panic room, I saw Jenny sitting there with her feet up on a chair with a paper script in her hand. She looked rather stressed]. She asked me "what the hell" was going on in the specific campaign where the numbers were a disaster. She told me that there was a lot of pressure from upstairs and as the quarter would end in two days, the campaign would have to be finished no matter what. [Campaigns always need to be finished within the quarter for financial and legal reasons and because new campaigns start at the beginning of the new quarter]. She asked me what the problem was on the campaign. My reply was that the data were not very good and the topic of the script was not very interesting either. However, I added that I knew that we could not do anything about this because the script comes from the client and agents need to read from it. [Knowing that she was sometimes funny about saying out loud that agents change the script from the client, I didn't tell her that I had already tried to "spice up the script" a bit under the radar to improve the statistics. Although she often said one needs to improve the script, I played innocent to see how she'd react to the situation. Because of her constant flip-flopping, some team leaders called her two-faced.]

In this situation, she got angry with me and said that in a case like this I need to change the script—I should have known that. Then, she went on complaining about sales and said that the script should have never been sold like this. This script was an example of sales trying to land a client. The entire campaign had always been unrealistic and sales upstairs should have never agreed to it as then we would not be in this mess in the first place. She should always be present when a campaign is sold to ensure that a good campaign is sold. However, now that we were at the end of the quarter, hitting the numbers by any means was more important than following the "client's script." According to her, if the numbers weren't hit, everyone in the call center would be in more trouble than I could possibly imagine.

Jenny knew it was not possible to read straight from the script, although she would never admit to that openly. As she told me, "Do you really think I don't know that agents don't follow the script word for word? I'm not blind or deaf and I have been on the phone too once." However, she believed it was dangerous to tell agents that they could ignore the script although she knew that most did. Officially, her line was that agents need to read from the script. She added that the client would also not be very happy if they found out that people who know very little about IT (and only after a few hours training), possibly not native speakers, called up a client's

(continued)

(continued)

target and conducted customer service, marketing, and sales on their behalf without a script or not reading from it. But right now, between them at that moment, for this campaign, she did not care about following the script but just about hitting the targets. Her suggestion was for me to give agents a few tips on how they could make the script more interesting and they could take a few notes. She warned me, though, that I needed to be discreet about this. Neither the operations manager nor anyone from upstairs should hear or see me doing this as they would not be happy about it and would not understand.

Aims and scope

The call center is perhaps the archetype of a contemporary workplace in (i) conditions of employment, (ii) recruitment, (iii) standardization practices, (iv) global reach and communication, and (v) surveillance. I focus on effects of call center employment on the lives of employees in the workplace, on their productivity, and on individual reactions to scripts within the workplace. This includes not only call center agents working the lines, but also call center managers directly responsible for implementing campaigns, and their corporate managers who negotiate agreements and targets with clients. Taking a linguistic ethnographic approach, this book is the first to explore the complexities of such work for employees, the expertise required, and the management of production across diverse levels of the organization.

The central argument of the book is that understanding the role of a calling script reveals the dynamics of the workplace. The approach I take therefore examines the "career of a calling script" as it travels through the organization. Along the way it becomes clear how such scripts, as corporate documents, exemplify the standardization of workplace language, of practice generally, and of practices of creative agency. I argue that standardization is both central to people's work and requires forms of expertise that go beyond what has been acknowledged in the training literature and academic writing on call centers. Questions I address in this book are: How is standardization accomplished across the organization through scripting? What does it mean for the people involved? What are the challenges they face? How do they make sense of this process and work with it?

The overarching message of the book is that while standardization is increasingly pervasive in the contemporary workplace, and has been the focus of ongoing critique, the challenges for workers in these environments arises not so much from scripts as from processes of daily target setting that create pressures for agents as they must achieve these goals to stay in their jobs. This is further compounded by issues of stigmatization of their work and the expertise required to accomplish it. My analysis shows that previous studies have oversimplified standardization in outbound call centers by focusing attention narrowly on the dynamics of control and resistance instead of exploring how scripts are actually produced, taken up, used, and interpreted by call center agents. Such studies have ignored both the benefits of standardization and the subtle forms of agency that occur in practice in the workplace.

The context

This book draws largely on my long-term participant ethnographic fieldwork undertaken in a multilingual call center. The call center that will be the focus of this book is located in London, a quintessential global city. The term *global city* was coined by Saskia Sassen and is now widely used to denote a few cities "that are strategic sites in the global economy because of their concentration of command functions and high-level producer-service firms oriented to world markets" (Sassen 1994, 145). London's status as a global city and as a hub of the global service economy is often linked to its financial services; not many think of London as a call center hub. However, the stigmatized, less glamorous, and often overlooked parts of the service industries, such as the call centers, also play an important role in the service economy. In fact, perhaps surprisingly to many, London is home to the pan-European call center industry, as many headquarters host their multilingual call centers there to coordinate incoming and outgoing calls from across Europe. A recent survey by the government on the British call center industry suggests that around the turn of the millennium, the call center phenomenon began to penetrate the consciousness of the British public, as these institutions expanded on an unprecedented level for businesses and consumers and began outsourcing call centers to other English-speaking countries (DTI 2004, 9). This expansion has led to over one million workers in UK call centers ("Contact Centre Operations: Labour Market Report" 2012, 5). It has been estimated that up to four percent of the British population work in call centers. When it comes to the question of what actually makes a call center, McPhail (2002) provides a useful definition.

> A call center is a specialized office, where agents [spending all their working days primarily on the phone] remotely provide information, deliver services and/or conduct sales, using some combination of integrated telephone and information technologies, typically with an aim of enhancing customer service while reducing organizational costs. (McPhail 2002, 10)

Usually, a further distinction is made between outbound and inbound call centers. This book focuses on an outbound multilingual IT call center. Agents in outbound call centers make only outbound calls and may carry out a range of functions: fund-raising, survey research, telemarketing, and telesales. Such activities are not so much services but sales-oriented activities (McPhail 2002, 18). The call center I focus on here offers a range of services from marketing to customer service and telesales, but most work is related to telemarketing.

Background: call centers, standardization, scripts

Call center research has been interdisciplinary and has included sociologists, scholars of management studies, sociolinguists, and linguistic anthropologists cross-referencing one another. Many of these studies focus on standardization (cf. Belt et al. 2000, 367–368). In fact, a survey of the interdisciplinary literature suggests that the majority of studies on call centers center on standardization. Academics have studied call centers predominately in a critical manner, with standardization as the main point of controversy and criticism (cf. Woydack 2014).

Following Timmermans and Epstein's (2010, 71) detailed review article of sociological theorizations of standardization. I define *standardization* here as "a process of constructing uniformities across time and space, through the generation of agreed-upon rules" as well as guidelines. Call centers, as Belt et al. (2002, 28) point out, are designed to be "environment[s] in which work can be standardized to create relatively uniform and repetitive activities so as to achieve economies of scale and consistent quality of customer service." Taylorist methods, based on those developed by Frederick Taylor to improve economic efficiency in manufacturing industries in the late nineteenth and early twentieth century, have been adapted in call center labor management. As Holtgrewe and colleagues (2002, 1) note, "call centers are the area of front-line information work, which most closely approximates the model of regimented or Taylorised service work organization (Frenkel et al. 1998; Taylor and Bain 1999)." However, it is presumed that standardization is largely achieved in call centers through scripts rather than the assembly line. Scripts are designed to control agents' speech and

> are carefully structured to manage the [agent's phone] transaction in the most efficient way, not only to achieve organizational targets, and also to present a branded, corporate persona [but also]... [at the same time] such scripting is designed to achieve process goals of sequencing, clarity, rapport building, and branding, and task goals that include information gathering, information giving, information accuracy, and sales. (Houlihan 2003, 150)

Cameron (2000b) has suggested that in fact this practice has led to three types of standardization: scripting entire conversations, prompting, and staging. In a script "the provision of a full specification" is made "for every word uttered by the operator" (Cameron 2000a, b, 330). In this case, agents are no longer authors of their talk, but only "animators" (Goffman 1981). In the second type, some call centers make use of "a prompt sheet which specifies what interactional moves the operator should make in what order, but do not prescribe a standard form of words" (Cameron 2000b, 330). Finally, some call centers provide "only general guidelines for the 'staging' of a transaction, leaving the exact number of moves in each stage to the operator's discretion" (2000b, 330). In this case, the corporation achieves a standard not in *what* their agents say, but more importantly in *how* they say it (2000b, 331). This would include for instance having to deliver a script in a "smiley voice." This move seems to be fairly common and is enforced by strict monitoring (cf. e.g., Cameron 2000a, b, 331; Tomalin 2010, 182).

In 2008, Cameron further observed that scripting entire conversations had become *the* dominant type of standardization. Accordingly, scripts are imposed "top- down" (Cameron 2008, 143) and are coupled with high tech monitoring that not only records calls but also tracks every click that agents make on their computers. Because of these practices, call centers are likened to Foucault's panopticon (cf. Taylor and Bain 1999; Bain and Taylor 2000; Fernie and Metcalf 1998). As Bain and Taylor note, the panopticon metaphor has become the dominant metaphor for call center work in academia and the press (2000, 3). As in a panopticon, agents work in an electronic prison in which every step they make is recorded and can be monitored, and agents are aware of this.

Although the standardization of service work, such as the use of scripts and monitoring, was not unheard of in the past, the spread of standardization within the service economy is new (cf. on telephone operators Norwood 1990; Green 2001). Leidner links this development to the fact that the cost and quality of interactive work is more important in the new economy (1993, 24). As a result, Leidner suggests, it has become attractive to try out principles of standardization devised originally for application in manufacturing work in service industries that depend on human interaction. It is argued that standardization in these industries should allow for lower labor costs because of the increasing repetitiveness of the job and increased managerial control. While for Leidner the standardization in manufacturing is designed to "assure a uniform outcome and to make the organization less dependent on the skills of individual workers," she notes that in "interactive service work routinization [standardization] cannot [be] so readily accomplish[ed] (...)" (1993, 24). For instance, quality control in interactive service jobs not only involves standardizing products, but imagines standardizing the employees themselves. As Leidner writes, "this involves extending organizational control to aspects of the workers' selves that are usually considered matters of personal choice or judgement" (1993, 24–25). Therefore, the new nature of service work and the tendency to impose on individual selves raises questions about whether standardization is morally and psychologically justifiable. According to Leidner, such questions arise not only in respect to service workers but also with respect to service recipients whose behavior may be standardized to some degree.

The scholarly literature is consistent in finding "scripted Taylorism" highly problematic (Mirchandani 2012, 86–88) as a dehumanizing mode of standardization accompanied by panoptic monitoring. One criticism leveled at scripts is that they lead to deskilling of employees; scripts create "assembly lines in the head" turning "workers into robots" as they reduce agents' capacities to solve problems and make independent decisions (Taylor and Bain 1999; cf. e.g., Ritzer 1998, 64; Korczynski 2002, 43; Cameron 2000a, 98). Others propose that "call center workers (…) experience scripts as de-skilling, repetitive, and tedious" (Mirchandani 2012, 87). Cameron blames scripts and their associated monitoring for making call centers a "deskilling and disempowering place to work" (2000a, 124).

However, the vast diversity of call centers has received little attention. Calling agents in different companies can work with varied levels of discretion, skill, teamwork, pay, training, monitoring, and educational qualification (Batt and Moynihan 2002). Sallaz describes an inbound call center in which "agents encounter so many different types of calls that no manageable set of routines could encompass them all" (2015, 12). Organizational structures vary as well.

Researchers rarely take this perspective in the call center literature. They often lump diverse kinds of call centers together into one category as the archetype of the standardized workplace. Call centers' bad reputation is reflected in metaphors such as "communication factories" (Cameron 2000a, 93); "electronic panopticons" (Bain and Taylor 2000, 5), and "the new sweatshops" (Fernie and Metcalf 1998, 2) to name a few. As a result of the circulation of these images, Holman and Fernie (2000) have noted that call centers "conjure up an image of oppressive, stifling working conditions, constant surveillance, and poor job satisfaction" (2000, 1).

I argue in this book that much of the academic call center literature reflects a wider pattern in research on workplace standardization (see also Woydack and Rampton 2016). In a recent sociology review article on the history of standardization/standards, the authors note the apparent contradiction between two etymologically related terms: *standards* and *standardization*. Standards tend to be regarded as desirable, something one strives to achieve. However, standardization in popular usage tends to have negative connotations as in the imposition of industrial uniformity as opposed to individuality (2010, 71). This perspective is rooted in the intellectual foundations of social theory dating to Karl Marx and Max Weber in which standardization is interpreted as negative, leading to homogeneity, deskilling, and dehumanization. Timmermans and Epstein (2010, 71) argue that "the derogatory connotation [of standardization] persists." They argue that it is, for instance, encapsulated in Ritzer's McDonaldization-of-society thesis (2000), "as well as by much writing that views the standardization of people as inherently dehumanizing" (2010, 71). Although Foucault did not use the term, Timmermans and Epstein further suggest that Foucault, like Marx and Weber before him, believed standardization was a powerful means to regulate society. However, Foucault shared with Marx and Weber a critical concern with top-down structural designs oriented toward promoting uniformity. He also tended "to emphasize the link between standardization and the homogenization or flattening of social life in modernity" (Timmermans and Epstein 2010, 74).

Against this long-standing historical background described by Timmermans and Epstein, Leidner (1993, 5) observes that researchers, accepting the stigmatization of standardization, celebrate workers who make changes to scripts. Such individuals, it is assumed, must be acting in resistance to the oppression of standardization out of discontentment. Most authors further write under the assumption that resistance is risky for call center employees. Call centers are characterized by employment practices that have shifted the risk from employer to employee. It is common practice for call centers to employ workers on flexible short-term contracts and to not allow trade unions, meaning that if workers resist standardization practices, they may find themselves immediately without a job. Moreover, Mumby (2005, 26), in an extensive study of the service sector, adds that studies of resistance taking either neo-Marxist or Foucauldian approaches, despite the wide epistemological divide between them, tend to explore resistance in a dualistic framework of control and resistance. Giddens's (1979) conceptualization of agency "as the ability to act otherwise" goes largely unnoticed by researchers in their studies of call center practices.

In line with Mumby's analysis, Leidner (1993) notes that existing accounts tend to overstate the employer's success in imposing standardization practices on employees and assume that these practices serve the goals of management. Little attention, she concludes, for both theoretical and methodological reasons, is paid to workers' subjectivities or more subtle accounts of resistance.

Theoretically, studies of call centers have failed to go beyond an a priori conception of the dynamics of control and resistance. Methodologically, call center researchers have found it difficult to observe call center agents during their routines or to interview management in ways that would transcend this overused theoretical framework. Observational studies on call centers are the exception but so far these have been limited in various ways. Cameron (2000a) provides a convincing account of why researchers do not tend to conduct observational studies in call centers or interview agents, referring to the problem of access to their workers and the shop floor:

> At the time of my research there had recently been a number of critical press reports about working conditions in British call centers, and some managers were wary of my approaches. Often they were eager to show me their centers which they felt had been unfairly criticized, but reluctant to let me talk to their staff unchaperoned, and insistent on approving what I wrote in advance of publication (…). (2000a, 184)

Only a few studies have involved participant observation and these often have critical problems. Houlihan (2003), working from the perspective of management studies, took on the role of customer service representative and conducted undisclosed participant observation for one year of her two-year research project. Ethically, this is questionable research practice. Although she writes about scripts and notes that some agents change them as a way to resist, her insights do not include actual examples of how this is done or examples of transformative agency. In another study, Brannan conducted fieldwork for thirteen months (2005).

Even though Brannan's project focus was on sexuality within internal team dynamics and the management was aware of that, he originally told the informants and co-workers that his research was about the daily routines of the call center. He feared that his study could be misinterpreted by his co-workers "as an official investigation of Customer Service Representative (CSR) misbehavior" (2005, 425). Subsequently, he left his call center job, but re-entered the field to conduct follow-up interviews to confirm his status as a researcher and inform informants of the true nature of his research. Brannan's study focused only on sexuality within internal team dynamics and did not address transformative practices or the constraints of standardization. Sallaz conducted a study lasting six months (2015) and Roy carried out research but for only four months (2003); both studies were perhaps too brief to yield subtle data on transformative practices. Sallaz's study focused on what motivates agents to work harder in call centers. He only briefly writes about scripts, saying that "agents encounter so many different types of calls that no manageable set of routines could encompass them all" (2015, 12), and it is the challenge of learning the job that "motivates agents to work as hard as they do" (2015, 26). In fact, he continues that "[b]y far, the most common complaint I heard from workers was that management provided them too little guidance on how to handle their call" (Sallaz 2015, 26; see also Woydack and Rampton 2016).

Roy's (2003) study goes into more detail about scripts in bilingual call centers in Canada. She finds that agents have to read from scripts to qualify for a bonus system, which means inflexibility for agents in responding to customers' needs on the phone. Moreover, having to read from a standardized French script devalues the varieties of French Canadian that agents speak. But her account does not include examples from these standardized scripts, information on how they were written, or how this would differ from what agents would say in their own varieties of French. It is not clear what they actually say on the phone and whether following the script truly means following it verbatim, or whether there is some room for variation. Instead she focuses on the beliefs and language ideologies that surround the call center's hiring and operational practices.

In a similar vein, Duchêne's research on a Swiss multilingual call center (2009) focused on the language ideologies and tensions that govern the local call center. His fieldwork lasted ten days. He briefly mentions that there are scripts with greetings in every language, but does not describe how they are used. Other researchers indicate using participant observation methods but do not specify the duration of their fieldwork, making it difficult to assess the outcomes (e.g., Alarcón and Heyman 2013). Alarcón and Heyman (2013) researched linguistic practices in bilingual American call centers on the Mexican border. Again, they do not focus on agents' transformative practices in their use of scripts, although they state that in some cases agents need not follow a script (cf. Alarcón and Heyman 2013, 13). Besides the difficulty of access to the floor to observe people during their work routines, Taylor and Bain (1999) note difficulties in interviewing management.

Perhaps because of the difficulty in conducting semi-structured open interviews, call center studies in industrial sociology, the field from which most call center studies stem, typically rely on questionnaires. Questionnaires by nature predetermine all categories of inquiry. Questions reflect researchers' preconceived hypotheses rather than opening up opportunities for issues to emerge from their subjects. It is ironic that investigations targeting standardization depend on standardized questionnaires that limit the dynamics that can be explored. For instance, asking agents about key stressors in the work environment as determined by researchers may show how agents respond to researchers' categories. But it does not reveal what the agents might spontaneously relate as their own concerns. Although questionnaires can provide an overall idea of some of the issues related to standardization, they cannot explain wider complexities such as contradictory perceptions of standardization among staff members. Moreover, in responding to questionnaires, agents may feel the need to reproduce strong negative discourses condemning standardization given the public's negative perception of it, while in daily practice their activities may be more complex and less clear cut. Therefore, I propose that taking a detailed long-term linguistic ethnographic approach may be a more thorough means of enquiry, as ethnography produces in-depth accounts that reveal subjective stances and offer the rich data needed to allow a researcher to "establish theoretically valid connections between events and phenomena" that may have gone unnoticed or unaccounted for in prior studies (Mitchell 1984, 239).

This study differs from a traditional ethnography because it took place in the UK and because I was not an outsider. Nevertheless, as the urban ethnographies by the Chicago School from the 1920s showed (e.g., Thomas and Znaniecki 1927), research taking an insider perspective can be insightful. That is, the Chicago school's studies were significant, as these researchers investigated "face-to-face interaction in everyday settings, and produced descriptive narratives of social worlds" (O'Reilly 2009, 31). More specifically, according to Deegan, these ethnographers "often lived in the settings studied, walked the streets, collected qualitative and quantitative data, worked for local agencies, and had autobiographical experiences emerging from these locals or ones similar to them" (2001, 20). O'Reilly (2009) further notes that the ethnographers of "the Chicago school not only got out into the streets in their own cities and communities, but they were in many cases personally involved in the lives and lifestyles of those they studied" (2009, 110). The Chicago sociologists' work was therefore important, as it did not follow the "outsider paradigm" often prioritized in ethnographic studies. For O'Reilly (2009), these "insider" studies benefited from the fact that

> insiders (…) blend in more, gain more rapport, participate more easily, have more linguistic competence with which to ask more subtle questions on more complex issues, and are better at reading non-verbal communications. (…) They get beyond the ideal to the real, daily lived, and back-stage experiences. Rather than describing the unconscious grammar of the community, their ethnographies are expressions of it, the result of a superior insider knowledge gained through primary socialization. (2009, 114)

In this book I take a linguistic ethnographic approach (cf. Rampton et al. 2015). Rather than simple ethnography, I focus on linguistic behavior as much of the standardization in the form of scripting is linked to language. It is widely believed by researchers that language is a crucial managerial tool for controlling workers. However, I argue that the relationship between workers and scripts has not been adequately revealed in previous research as a result of the lack of long-term fieldwork. Houlihan claims in her ethnography, for instance, that except for a subversive ritual that agents call the "banana game" in which they compete with one another over how often they can get the word banana into a call unspotted by the customer, scripts are followed verbatim (2003, 137). Similarly, Cameron notes that informants "reported taking liberties with their scripts and ignoring instructions to smile" (2000a, 113), but readers are not provided with any detail on how scripts are manipulated to reflect that "smile." This is the kind of detail that is needed to understand the vignette described in the beginning of this chapter. Why do managers react differently in different contexts, and how do agents think about scripts and standardization in ways that go beyond the binary of control and resistance and that transcend the negative imagery that emerged from previous research?

With this book I demonstrate that scripts are open to transformation in the minds and practices of middle level management and agents in call centers, and that, contra most of the literature, call center workers are less subservient and drilled than has been argued. I explore how scripts are adapted and annotated at key points as they travel along the call center's organizational structure, with all staff displaying agency—*agency* defined here as the ability to "act otherwise" (Giddens 1984, 14) beyond strict client constraints and beyond the given syntax and lexicon of scripts handed down from upper level management (see also Woydack and Rampton 2016). Importantly, I show in what follows that the acts of transformation by agents and call floor managers are not resistance, but rather instances of appreciation of structural guidelines intertwined with situational flexibility in implementing goals. This dynamic intermingling of structure and transformation highlights the complexity of creative compliance and subtle agency beyond open resistance. Below I bring theory and method for this research together in a syncretic design for understanding call center labor.

Theoretical framing and methodological designs intertwined

The perspective on transposition or the mutability of texts that stems from linguistic anthropology combined with a focus on institutional ethnography serves as the central theoretical framework for this research. Neither has previously been used in framing call center studies. Institutional ethnography centers texts in the processes of "objectification of organizations" and examines the ways in which texts "mediate, regulate, and authorize people's activities" within institutions (Smith 2001, 160) even across long distances in an increasingly globalized world (Anderson 2004, 145; Farrell 2001, 190).

The study of institutional texts is significant because, as Smith notes, "from a particular text it is possible to trace sequences of actions through the institutional paths identifying where and how the institutional texts produce the standardized controls of everyday work activities" (2001, 160). That is, following a text trajectory across an organization allows for studying ruling relations and standardization within an organization. In her work, Smith (1996, 2001) shows not only how the material text creates "the join" (Smith 1996, 176) in today's global workforce between workers and institutions but also that texts play a key role in making standardization possible. She traces the emergence of standardization to science experiments and workplace/accounting practices that began in the early twentieth century. A key contribution is said to have been made by Robert Boyle, whose detailed instructions on the technology of the air pump made it possible (in principle) to replicate the experimental machine and experimental procedure, which thus "standardized events at different times and in different places" (Smith 1996, 181). Although Boyle's experiment of identical replication was not entirely successful, Smith (1996) writes that it created the conditions for subsequent standardization in science and at work. Moreover, in the early twentieth century, accounting and accountancy began to emerge as the "actual organizer[s] of the relations articulating people's work, particularly the processes of production and sales but also of management (...)" (1996, 182), which also coincided with the rise of stock markets. The local order of the shop floor thus became increasingly regulated by material/accounting technology that according to Smith created (for management) and imposed on workers "a local order of accountability fully compatible with and interpretable in terms of the corporate system of accounting" (Smith 1996, 183).

Even Taylorism produced "a standardization of work practices that will correspond to the systematics of the accounting text" (1996, 184). Farrell adds that in today's economy, monitoring, control (and standardization) are primarily text-based (2009, 190). For example, to monitor their employees, many firms now take advantage of textual aspects of work by using new technology that records every key stroke they enter into their computers. She also notes that "the coercive effect of call center operators being required to read their screen, and follow a script without deviating, even where this involves assuming a different cultural identity (either implicitly or explicitly) is now well documented" (e.g., Mirchandani 2004 cited in Farrell 2009, 190).

Farrell's observation helps to explain why calling scripts have become the main source of controversy in the academic debate on standardization. Smith and institutional ethnographers are, however, not alone in investigating trajectories of texts across institutions. More recently, anthropologists and literacy theorists have started following the trajectories of texts and their transposition and have made some important contributions. Possibilities for transposition highlight the fluidity of texts as they move through participants and across their trajectories. Scripts consist of multiple transportable textual units, some of which may flow easily across categories of participants while others are subject to reformulation as new actors interpret them. This synthesis creates a novel theoretical framework that allows me to transcend the dualism of control and resistance to investigate the nuanced transformations of scripts in use. By focusing on "flows" or "chains" of texts and texts as mobile, the framework allows me to conduct a multi-sided ethnography in line with post-modern theorizations (cf. Marcus 1995, 105) although I only visited one physical field site.

This book is a case study of "CallCentral" (a pseudonym), a typical outbound call center located in London in the south-east of England. IT issues are the focus of business with clients. I give special attention to two processes in CallCentral's activities: entextualization and recontextualization. *Entextualization* involves selecting, designing, and inscribing prose for a text that will travel into other settings where recipients implement it.

Recontextualization describes the possible ways these meanings and forms are adapted, construed, and altered in the process of interpretation by the text's recipient. Because of the emphasis on deskilling and standardization in the literature, I focus on alterations and adaptations by downstream users of a script. In Chapters 3, 4 and 5 I describe the processes by which a calling script is entextualized and then recontextualized. Chapter 3 describes how clients and upper level management co-produce a master script. In Chapter 4 I examine recontextualization of the script as call center managers and team leaders explain the document to their call agents. Chapter 5 examines how agents themselves make sense of the script, recontextualizing it again to use it on the phone. Each chapter traces in detail the transformations a script undergoes as it moves from production by corporate management and clients to the call center floor. I explore the authority of the scripts, the appreciation for the organization and order they provide, as well as the orientations of managers and agents (Bauman 1996) toward personalizing the document, insuring time for listening, and incorporating politeness strategies. These foci allow me to address issues highlighted in previous literature on standardization and are crucial to the ways researchers have approached script-based call centers.

CallCentral is part of a larger global multinational media corporation. Employees make calls on behalf of external clients using any of the world's languages the client requests. Typically, at least 20 different languages are being used at any one time across all campaigns in the call center. Calls are often made to countries outside Europe, including South Africa, countries in the Middle East, and the United States. The center has on average 60 seats and about five call center managers. The exact number of agents working in the call center depends on the demand for campaigns.

CallCentral is an outbound call center heavily reliant on calling scripts and differs in this respect from inbound call centers such as the one described by Sallaz (2015). My experience with CallCentral spans four years in which I was an agent on the phone and worked as a trainer as well. I conducted participant observation for three years as part of my research. Considering the opportunity to review and improve the working efficiency of their center, management were happy to approve my participant- observation research. I always informed agents of my research as I trained or otherwise engaged with them.

I interviewed 60 members of the CallCentral staff including three call center managers, six team leaders, and current, new, and former agents. All informants signed consent forms and received summaries of the goals and procedures of the research project as approved by the IRB of King's College London where this research was conducted. All subjects mentioned in this book have been guaranteed anonymity through the creation of pseudonyms. I used semi-structured interviews to provide bases for comparison that still allowed individuals to expand on topics in ways I might not have anticipated. I included a wide range of topics in my questioning from local standardization practices to general perceptions and impressions of call centers. We addressed the whys and wherefores of how they ended up working in a call center and the specifics of their practices. Interviews were conducted either in a location outside the call center itself but in the same building, or at venues chosen by the participant (e.g., at home or in a café).

Scripts are the heart of this book since, as the next chapter demonstrates, they are the link between different levels of the organization's hierarchy and a primary source of controversy surrounding call centers' standardization practices. They also underpin the operational side of the call center itself. CallCentral has a high turnover. Almost 20 new agents start every week and there are constant staff shortages. Few agents have backgrounds in IT, the focus of the call center's business. During the years of my research, scripts outlined what agents were expected to articulate on the phone by clients and by management at the highest levels. They were used for training, they made quantitative and qualitative monitoring possible, and they were fed into the compilation of company statistics (cf. also Woydack and Rampton 2016).

Outline of the book

With this book I aim to develop a better understanding of perceptions and practices of standardization by workers and managers in call centers. Detailed participant- observation has allowed me to reject the position that the standardization of call center work and its effect on the human personality is entirely negative. Some manipulations might be infantilizing, invasive, and demeaning, but to understand standardization practices in call center work and how workers and managers perceive them, a more precise account is necessary, one that draws on a variety of methods including participant observation and following the trajectory of a script.

As I develop the book, I describe the three stages every script in CallCentral passes through. I focus on an anonymized but highly typical client whose project is similar to actual projects I witnessed in terms of the production, adaptation, and enactment of a set of working scripts. Before I go into the details of the campaign and the actual "career of a script," I provide background detail on CallCentral and show how the theories and methods explained so far apply to this case study.

In Chapter 2 I present some of my impressions and observations of the field site and draw on interviews to showcase agents' perspectives. I open by introducing the employees and their daily routines. Then I look through the eyes of a typical new agent on their first day. I critique the impression given in the scholarly literature of call centers exclusively as sites of standardization. I highlight the partial accuracy of accounts of standardization and reveal unpredictable elements of the organization, how it is run, and how agents' performances undermine uniformity. The first section serves as a commentary on the mix of standardization, unpredictability, and relaxation in the organization; the second shows how individuals articulate these tensions.

From conception to use, scripts go through three main stages reflecting CallCentral's organizational hierarchy. In each stage, the respective staff face a production and accountability system. Chapter 3 presents the first stage—the production of the script by the client, corporate management, and the campaign manager. This phase is marked by disagreement among the various parties because of their contrasting notions of what a script should be. The benefit of the trajectory approach is that it shows how the campaign managers create a "durable and authoritative" reference text which the client agrees on. Corporate management and the client dictate that the script should be read verbatim so that accurate statistics can be produced, the main production of accountability on this level. The script is meant to regulate agents "downstairs." However, it becomes clear that this static view of the script read verbatim is limited to "upstairs" corporate management and company clients. Campaign managers display a different rationality and know that the script will be transformed and transpositioned as soon as it travels to the call center.

Chapter 4 depicts the transfer of a script to the team leaders' level and focuses on how campaign managers and team leaders draw on the script during agent training. We see that the overall structure of the script, in this case one with eight sections, remains intact and there is monitoring in place to enforce replication. However, as team leaders make sense of the training they receive from campaign managers about the key points of the script, they individually decide what the script's key points are, how to personalize it, and which words will travel well to agents and call recipients.

I show specific examples of the script's transformation and team leaders' motivations for those. The individual transpositions of the team leader's versions of the script are used for their training of agents. During training, team leaders then tell agents within which parameters (the eight-section approach) they can make transpositions to the script. Here I also observe the complexities of the corporate hierarchy and of the diverse subjectivities within the company. While normally these differences are juggled well and overcome by campaign managers, sometimes they surface in the open and cause conflict.

Chapter 5 examines the final phase in which agents translate a script into other languages and work with it on the phone, engaging in detailed data logging to record their calls so the logs can be fed back to the management and the client. Data logging is a primary activity for call agents at this stage and indirectly contributes to potential transformations in scripts. Agents display a great deal of agentive action when it comes to the transformation of the script in line with the sanctioned parameters of the eight-section approach. They spend a lot of time personalizing the script prior to calling. Then they adapt it further on the phone as they receive feedback through recipient responses, applying textual transformative strategies from a plurality of influences.

Agents appreciate the script as a tool they can refashion for their own use within set parameters and try their best to do so. Far from oppressing agents, scripts help them comply creatively with company standards and campaign goals. Typically unaware of the upper level management's mandate that scripts be read verbatim, agents balance structure and situational

demands to achieve their goals. However, the targets set for agent performance are not always reasonable and agents often object to the high dial
rates they have to meet every day. These goals, too, are subject to efforts
at manipulation even while the agents work hard to achieve company
goals. The corporate and call center managements are aware that the dial
rates are impossible to meet. They see unobtainable dial rates as a managerial strategy to incentivize agents to work harder in their efforts to meet
them. In this chapter I describe the demands of data logging, and how
data logging is a primary activity of call agents in terms of accountability.
It also leads to potential transformations in scripts.

In Chapter 6 I summarize the contributions of this work and discuss
its implications. I show that ethnographic fieldwork is essential to unrav-
eling the role of standardization practices through the textual tools
required by call center service work. I investigate how details from the
fieldwork and interviews connect with broader issues such as the increasing impact of technology and standardization (audit cultures) on workers
and the workplace, resistance versus compliance, conceptualizations of
agency, learning and training in the workplace (upskilling and deskilling), diversity and language management, language commodification,
and stigma associated with low-skilled workplaces. Rather than simply
analyzing agents' call transcripts, I address here the range of practices by
call center staff at various levels, investigating what happens inside this
secretive industry by taking into account every hierarchical level and their
mutual influences.

The theoretical framework I adopt—a new synthesis of transposition
and organizational ethnography—offers insight into organizational and
corporate processes of textual production and use. The framework builds
upon and expands previous work from literacy studies (cf. Baynham and
Prinsloo 2009). I refer to this new theoretical framework as "institutional
transpositional ethnography." The book aims to offer fresh perspectives
on how to ethnographically study a corporation, especially a call center,
to reveal the dynamics of standardization, audit culture(s), agency, conceptualizations of resistance, and creative compliance.

References

Alarcón, Amado, and Josiah McC. Heyman. 2013. Bilingual Call Centers at the US- Mexico Border: Location and Linguistic Markers of Exploitability. *Language in Society* 42 (01): 1–21.

Anderson, Donald L. 2004. The Textualizing Functions of Writing for Organizational Change. *Journal of Business and Technical Communication* 18 (2): 141–164.

Bain, Peter, and Phil Taylor. 2000. Entrapped by the 'Electronic Panopticon'? Worker Resistance in the Call Centre. *New Technology, Work and Employment* 15 (1): 2–18.

Batt, Rosemary, and Lisa Moynihan. 2002. The Viability of Alternative Call Centre Production Models. *Human Resource Management Journal* 12 (4): 14–34.

Bauman, Richard. 1996. Transformations of the Word in the Production of Mexican Festival Drama. In *Natural Histories of Discourse*, ed. Michael Silverstein and Greg Urban, 301–329. Chicago/London: Chicago University Press.

Baynham, Mike, and Mastin Prinsloo, eds. 2009. *The Future of Literacy Studies. Palgrave Advances in Linguistics.* Basingstoke/New York: Palgrave Macmillan.

Belt, Vicki, Ranald Richardson, and Juliet Webster. 2000. Women's Work in the Information Economy: The Case of Telephone Call Centres. *Information, Communication & Society* 3 (3): 366–385.

———. 2002. Women, Social Skill and Interactive Service Work in Telephone Call Centres. *New Technology, Work and Employment* 17 (1): 20–34.

Brannan, Matthew J. 2005. Once More with Feeling: Ethnographic Reflections on the Mediation of Tension in a Small Team of Call Centre Workers. *Gender, Work and Organization* 12 (5): 420–439.

Cameron, Deborah. 2000a. *Good to Talk?* London: Sage.

———. 2000b. Styling the Worker: Gender and the Commodification of Language in the Globalized Service Economy. *Journal of Sociolinguistics* 4 (3): 323–347.

———. 2008. Talk from the Top Down. *Language & Communication* 28 (2): 143–155.

Contact Centre Operations: Labour Market Report. 2012. London: CFA@ business skills at work. http://www.oph.fi/download/145729_Contact_Centres_LMI_2012_.pdf

Deegan, Mary Jo. 2001. The Chicago School of Ethnography. In *Handbook of Ethnography*, ed. Paul Atkinson, Amanda Coffey, Sara Delamont, John Lofland, and Lyn Lofland, 11–23. London: Sage.

DTI. 2004. *The UK Contact Centre Industry: A Study*. London: Department of Trade and Industry.

Duchêne, Alexandre. 2009. Marketing, Management and Performance: Multilingualism as Commodity in a Tourism Call Centre. *Language Policy* 8 (1): 27–50.

Farrell, Lesley. 2001. Negotiating Knowledge in the Knowledge Economy: Workplace Educators and the Politics of Codification. *Studies in Continuing Education* 23 (2): 201–214.

———. 2009. Texting the Future: Work Literacies, New Economy and Economies. In *The Future of Literacy Studies*, ed. Mike Baynham and Mastin Prinsloo, 181–199. Basingstoke: Palgrave Macmillan.

Fernie, Sue, and David Metcalf. 1998. *(Not) Hanging on the Telephone: Payment Systems in the New Sweatshops*. London: London School of Economics, Centre for Economic Performance.

Frenkel, Stephen J., May Tam, Marek Korczynski, and Karen Shire. 1998. Beyond Bureaucracy? Work Organization in Call Centres. *The International Journal of Human Resource Management* 9 (6): 957–979.

Giddens, Anthony. 1979. *Central Problems in Social Theory: Action, Structure, and Contradiction in Social Analysis*. Berkeley: University of California Press.

———. 1984. *The Constitution of Society: Outline of the Theory of Structuration*. Berkeley: University of California Press.

Goffman, Erving. 1981. *Forms of Talk*, University of Pennsylvania Publications in Conduct and Communication. Philadelphia: University of Pennsylvania Press.

Green, Venus. 2001. *Race on the Line: Gender, Labor, and Technology in the Bell System, 1880–1980*. Durham: Duke University Press.

Holman, David, and Sue Fernie. 2000. Can I Help You? Call Centres and Job Satisfaction. *Centrepiece Magazine* 5 (1). http://cep.lse.ac.uk/centrepiece/v05i1/holman_fernie.pdf.

Holtgrewe, Ursula, Christian Kerst, and Karen Shire, eds. 2002. *Re-Organising Service Work: Call Centres in Germany and Britain*. Aldershot/Hants/Burlington: Ashgate.

Houlihan, Maeve. 2003. *Making Sense of Call Centres: Working and Managing the Front Line*. Unpublished, University of Lancaster, Lancaster.

Hudson, Alex. 2011. Are Call Centres the Factories of the 21st Century. *BBC News*.

Korczynski, Marek. 2002. *Human Resource Management in Service Work*, Management, Work and Organisations. Basingstoke: Palgrave Macmillan.

Leidner, Robin. 1993. *Fast Food, Fast Talk: Service Work and the Routinization of Everyday Life*. Berkeley: University of California Press.

Marcus, George E. 1995. Ethnography in/of the World System: The Emergence of Multi-Sited Ethnography. *Annual Review of Anthropology* 24 (1): 95–117.

McPhail, Brenda. 2002. *What Is 'on the Line' in Call Centre Studies? A Review of Key Issues on Academic Literature*. University of Toronto. http://www3.fis.utoronto.ca/research/iprp/publications/mcphail-cc.pdf.

Mirchandani, Kiran. 2004. Practices of Global Capital: Gaps, Cracks and Ironies in Transnational Call Centres in India. *Global Networks* 4 (4): 355–373.

———. 2012. *Phone Clones: Authenticity Work in the Transnational Service Economy*. Ithaca: ILR Press.

Mitchell, Clyde. 1984. Typicality and the Case Study. In *Ethnographic Research: A Guide to General Conduct*, ed. Roy Ellen, 238–241. London: Academic.

Mumby, Dennis K. 2005. Theorizing Resistance in Organization Studies: A Dialectical Approach. *Management Communication Quarterly* 19 (1): 19–44.

Norwood, Stephen H. 1990. *Labor's Flaming Youth: Telephone Operators and Worker Militancy, 1878–1923*, The Working Class in American History. Urbana: University of Illinois Press.

O'Reilly, Karen. 2009. *Key Concepts in Ethnography*, Sage Key Concepts. Los Angeles: Sage.

Power, Michael. 2010. *The Audit Society: Rituals of Verification*. Oxford: Oxford University Press, Reprinted.

Rampton, Ben, Janet Maybin, and Fiona Copland. 2015. Theory and Method in Linguistic Ethnography. In *Linguistic Ethnography: Interdisciplinary Explorations*, ed. Julia Snell, Sara Shaw, and Fiona Copland, 15–50. Basingstoke: Palgrave Macmillan.

Ritzer, George. 1998. *The McDonaldization Thesis: Explorations and Extensions*. London/Thousand Oaks: Sage.

———. 2000. *The McDonaldization of Society*. New Century ed. Thousand Oaks: Pine Forge Press.

Roy, Sylvie. 2003. Bilingualism and Standardization in a Canadian Call Center: Challenges for a Linguistic Minority Community. In *Language Socialization in Multilingual Societies*, ed. Robert Bayley and Sandra Schecter, 269–287. Clevedon: Multilingual Matters.

Sallaz, Jeffrey J. 2015. Permanent Pedagogy: How Post-Fordist Firms Generate Effort But Not Consent. *Work and Occupations* 42 (1): 3–34.

Sassen, Saskia. 1994. *Cities in a World Economy*, Sociology for a New Century. Thousand Oaks: Pine Forge Press.

Shore, Cris, and Susan Wright. 2015. Governing by Numbers: Audit Culture, Rankings and the New World Order: Governing by Numbers. *Social Anthropology* 23 (1): 22–28.

Smith, Dorothy E. 1996. The Relations of Ruling: A Feminist Inquiry. *Studies in Cultures, Organizations and Societies* 2 (2): 171–190.

———. 2001. Texts and the Ontology of Organizations and Institutions. *Studies in Cultures, Organizations and Societies* 7 (2): 159–198.

Sonntag, Selma K. 2009. Linguistic Globalization and the Call Center Industry: Imperialism, Hegemony or Cosmopolitanism? *Language Policy* 8 (1): 5–25.

Strathern, Marilyn, ed. 2000. *Audit Cultures: Anthropological Studies in Accountability, Ethics, and the Academy*, European Association of Social Anthropologists. London/New York: Routledge.

Taylor, Phil, and Peter Bain. 1999. 'An Assembly Line in the Head': Work and Employee Relations in the Call Centre. *Industrial Relations Journal* 30 (2): 101–117.

Thomas, William Isaac, and Florian Znaniecki. 1927. *The Polish Peasant in Europe and America: A Classic Work in Immigration History*. New York: Dover.

Timmermans, Stefan, and Steven Epstein. 2010. A World of Standards But Not a Standard World: Toward a Sociology of Standards and Standardization. *Annual Review of Sociology* 36 (1): 69–89.

Tomalin, Barry. 2010. India Rising: The Need for Two Way Training. In *Globalization. Communication and the Workplace*, ed. Gail Forey and Jane Lockwood, 172–190. London: Continuum.

Woydack, Johanna. 2014. *Standardisation and Script Trajectories in a London Call Centre: An Ethnography of a Multilingual Outbound Call Centre*. London: King's College London.

Woydack, Johanna, and Ben Rampton. 2016. Text Trajectories in a Multilingual Call Centre: The Linguistic Ethnography of a Calling Script. *Language in Society* 5 (05): 709–732.

2

Getting to Know CallCentral: A First Encounter

In this chapter I introduce CallCentral, its employees and its operations. I explain the centrality and importance of calling scripts to CallCentral's activities. The first part of the chapter provides a general background to the field site through the trope of a fictional agent's first day at work and explores some of the usual practices and attitudes among agents. The questions addressed include: What is an agent's workday like? What does working as a call center agent entail? What are the different roles within the call center? Who are the key people? How are agents recruited to call center work? The second part of the chapter draws on interviews with actual agents to explore why they joined the call center and their attitudes toward working there.

A fictional agent's first day at work

The call center is the second floor of a converted multi-story loft warehouse in central London. It is the only office on that floor. The entrance is simple, without a reception or company logo. Agents press a buzzer to enter, since call center doors remain closed and locked from the outside at all times. The call center supervisor or a team leader greets the new

© The Author(s) 2019   **27**
J. Woydack, *Linguistic Ethnography of a Multilingual Call Center:*
London Calling, Communicating in Professions and Organizations,
https://doi.org/10.1007/978-3-319-93323-8_2

agent and asks them to wait in the break area until everyone has arrived and their induction training can begin. All agents are hired as temporary workers. They must fill out the required paperwork, which includes a temporary contract. This states their pay and other terms such as layoffs without prior notice at the discretion of management and no sick leave. Some agents are hired through an agency for two weeks. In these cases the agency has completed the paperwork before their arrival at CallCentral. If the agent was hired via an agency, the call center will have been informed only the day before the agent comes to work. The information conveyed by the agency includes which language(s) the new employee speaks and has been tested on. It is unlikely that anyone from the call center will have seen a new agent's actual CV or know much else about their background.

The break out area, where agents wait for training to begin, is an open space with a few chairs and tables, and a pool table. From this area the new agent can see the call center, an open floor office with 60 seats. To shorten the wait and make them feel welcome, a team leader may show them to the kitchen, where they can make themselves a complimentary drink. Once the training starts, the group of new agents go to a meeting room. On average 20 new agents start every week. There, they are introduced to and learn about the company behind the call center and "systems training" begins.

Systems training is an introduction to the company's internal software, an integral part of call center work. This session usually lasts three hours, followed by lunch. After lunch, the new agents are divided into groups for their campaign training, where they are given their respective scripts and briefs, a written document that outlines details concerning the campaign, including the daily target expectations. There are two separate targets. "Lead targets" are the number of people a caller recruits to receive email, materials, or a call back from the client. "Dial rates" are how many calls agents have to make per day. On the brief, the agent learns how much they will be paid if they meet their weekly lead targets. Dial rates ensure that agents make as many calls as possible, because management believes that the more calls they make, the higher the likelihood they will make "leads." The campaign training lasts around 30 minutes and may take place in the "panic room," so named by the managers ironically because it is the only meeting room visible from the call center itself, allowing agents to observe the managers "panic" when a campaign goes awry.

When all the agents have received the campaign training, a team leader will teach them so-called soft skills for handling objections from interlocutors on the phone. A 30-minute session, an introduction to tips and tricks on the phone and objection handling, constitutes the final unit before they hit the floor. They are then assigned a seat where they familiarize themselves with the system and script as they make their first calls. At 5 pm, the team leader shows everyone how to log out of the company's internal computer software and how to sign off on their timesheet.

From this short account of an agent's first day, many questions emerge:

- Is there a seating order and what is the layout of the call center?
- How are agents monitored?
- What is systems training?
- What is campaign training?
- How are non-work related activities managed during the work day?
- Who are the key people in the call center?

Below, I cover these aspects of call center work in the same order as agents learn about them. That is, I start with the seating order and the layout of the call center.

The seating order and layout of the call center

Although the seating order in the call center is not fixed and there is a first-come, first-served policy, there are some general factors that determine where a new agent can sit. These tend to be linked to the organization's desire to monitor (electronically) new agents and those with (poor) reputations. After their first day, when new agents arrive the next morning and want to sit in the seat they had the first day, they realize that there is no fixed seating order, as someone else might be sitting in their previously "assigned seat." In that case, a team leader finds them a new one. After a while, new agents understand that some seats are reserved for team leaders and trusted agents who work on research-based campaigns;

those seats have full internet access. Other seats, those in positions that cannot be call monitored, are also not for new agents.

There are four "naughty seats" (the management's label) (Figure 2.1, seats 37–40), where the management puts agents who are considered lazy or otherwise in need of close monitoring. On their computer screens, management can see and hear what the faltering agents are doing.

New agents soon realize that there are other reasons for having no set seating order. Agents are moved onto different campaigns every day. Many work in the call center part time or only for short periods (two weeks or less). The constant changes in personnel undermine any attempts at a consistent seating pattern. From time to time, management makes an effort to seat agents together who are working on the same campaign/language/country, but this seating order is usually short-lived because other variables influence seating choices. An agent might want to sit close to peers and far away from the management. Some prefer sitting on the right because it is quieter with fewer rows and seats. Conversely, others favor the left side at the back, to be as far away from the management as possible. Many agents prefer workstations with older headsets over those with newer ones. Some agents have complained that the new headsets are so thick they block external sound and prevent chatting with one's neighbor.

Occasionally, when the call center operates at full capacity, the management deliberately calls in more agents than there are seats. The assumption is made, as with an overbooked flight, that many people will not show up on any given day and that most of the time there will be enough seats for everyone. This ensures that the call center operates at full capacity every day. However, sometimes at peak time more agents turn up than there are seats. With the first-come, first-served policy, those who come late and find no seats available are sent home unpaid. This is rare, however, since the turnover rate at CallCentral is very high. Agents stay on average only two weeks as they would have found a new job elsewhere.

As shown on the floor plan above (Figure 2.1), the call center consists of a large open-plan office, a break out area, three meeting rooms, a kitchen, and two toilets, all on one floor. Of the three meeting rooms, only one is still used solely for meetings: "the panic room," as the manager called it. The room itself is small and lacks computers. Agents are often summoned there for debriefs carried out by team leaders if managers are concerned

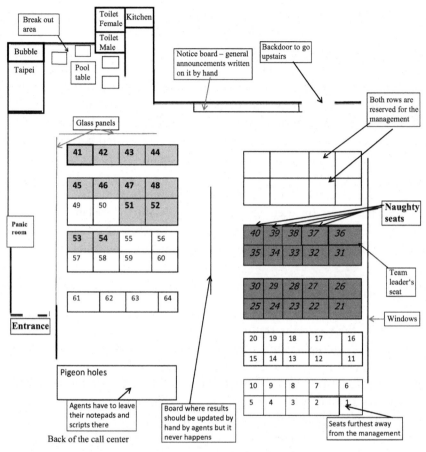

Break out area

Bubble

Taipei

Toilet Female

Toilet Male

Kitchen

Pool table

Notice board – general announcements written on it by hand

Backdoor to go upstairs

Both rows are reserved for the management

Glass panels

Panic room

Naughty seats

Team leader's seat

Windows

Entrance

Pigeon holes

Agents have to leave their notepads and scripts there

Back of the call center

Board where results should be updated by hand by agents but it never happens

Seats furthest away from the management

Key:

Seats (seats 41-48; 51-55) in bold = computers have internet access

Seats (21-40) in italics = cannot be monitored

Fig. 2.1 The layout of the call center

with their performance on a particular campaign. The room thus tends to signal the particular manager's "state of panic" as well as agents' fear of being summoned. It can be a calculated move for a manager to call an individual agent into the panic room or to have any kind of meeting in there, as this is visible to everyone. As a result, rumors often spread about why the summons or event took place.

The other two meeting rooms the managers call "Taipei" and "the bubble" are next to each another and are used for other purposes. "The bubble" is far from the noise and stress of the open-plan call center, hence putting its visitors in a bubble. Taipei, the largest of the meeting rooms, has many computers and is mostly used for training. If the call center has to operate at full capacity, agents might sit in Taipei to call. The smaller of these two meeting rooms, "the bubble," is the more exclusive one. This room is reserved for the call monitor and a few trusted agents to allow them privacy as managers have no visual access to the room and all computers have internet access.

The break out area in front of these two meeting rooms, where new agents take a seat on their first day, is important for socializing among agents, although some callers sit there for lunch and others play pool there. Both activities offer opportunities to meet fellow callers.

The hours of work

As part of their systems training, agents are told that CallCentral, on behalf of its external clients, offers project-based work. This entails contacting IT and business decision makers worldwide for marketing, customer service, and sales purposes. Agents call only businesses, never private households. Working hours are determined by the business working hours in the respective countries of the campaigns. Moreover, all call center work is temporary and campaign/project based. None of the agents, including the team leaders, have contracts; everyone is paid on an hourly basis. Their hourly rate ranges from £7.50 to £11.00 plus incentives. Agents are informed that their working hours depend on which country they are calling and the month of the year.

The month of the year is important for the organization of the call center, as some periods of the year are busier than others. The busiest times occur at the end of quarters. From a business point of view, the calendar year is divided into four quarters (each quarter has three months, e.g., 1 Jan–31 March). Given that budgets are allocated quarterly, a quarter functions as the time period within which campaigns have to be completed. So at the end of the quarter, the call center is very busy and agents are usually asked to work longer hours, since all campaigns must be completed by the last day of the quarter. The country the agent is calling and the time zone within that country are the other two decisive factors for agents' hours of work.

In practice this works out as follows. The normal working hours for the United Kingdom (GMT) are 09:00–17:00 Monday-Thursday and 09:00–16:00 Friday, with an hour lunch break from 12:30 to 13:30. For agents calling Germany, France, or Italy, for instance, countries one hour ahead of the UK, the normal work hours would be Mondays—Thursdays 08:30–16:30 and Fridays 08:30–16:00, with a lunch hour from 12:00 to 13:00. In Table 2.1 below I have summarized how the different time zones, the month of the quarter, along with the day can affect the agents' working hours.

Even though countries like Sweden, Spain, and the Benelux countries are in the same time zone as Germany and France, each of them have a local particularity that affects the calling hours, such as the siesta in Spain.

Table 2.1 Hours of work for agents

Country and time zone	UK+ Ireland, Portugal (GMT)	Germany, France, ZA, Italy +1 hour	Scandinavia and Benelux +1 hour	Spain +1 hour	Middle East + 4 hours	Russia- (European) +3 hours	USA East Coast +5 hours	USA West Coast +8 hours	Turkey + 2 hours
Start	09:00	08:30	08:30	08:30	08:30	08:30	12:30	17:00	08:30
Start time (end of quarter)	09:00	08:00	08:00	08:00	08:00	08:00	12:30	---	08:00
Break time	11:00 - 11:10	11:00 - 11:10	11:00 - 11:10	11:00 - 11:10	11:00 - 11:10	11:00	----	---	11:00 - 11:10
Lunch Time	12:30 - 13:30	12:00 - 13:00 (end of quarter 30min)	12:30 - 13:00	13:00 - 13:30	12:30 - 13:00	12:00 - 12:30	-----	-----	12:00 - 12:30
Afternoon break time	15:00 - 15:10	15:00 - 15:10	15:00 - 15:10	15:00 - 15:10	15:00 - 15:10	15:00 - 15:10	17:00 - 17:20	17:00 - 17:20	15:00 - 15:10
Finish	17:00	16:30	16:00	16:30	15:30	15:30	19:00	19:00	15:30
Finish time (end of quarter)	17:30	16:30	16:30	16:30			---	-----	
Finish time on Friday	16:00	16:00	16:00	16:00	15:30	15:30	16:00	16:00	15:30
Finish time on Friday (end of quarter)	16:30	16:00	16:00	16:00	15:30	15:30	16:00	16:00	15:30

The UK is the bench mark

In Scandinavia and Benelux, office hours tend to be shorter, thus the calling time is also shorter. Considering the "odd hours" and early finishing times of some regions in this schedule, it is common for agents to switch between countries on a given day. For instance, if an agent calls Switzerland, which has a countrywide lunch break from 11:00 to 12:30 (GMT), they might be asked to call Germany or France during the lunch period in Switzerland. This ensures that the contact rate for agents does not drop from 12 to 12:30 (GMT), when it is difficult to get hold of anyone, as most companies in the target country, in this case Switzerland, will be shut. Similarly, agents calling the Middle East may move to calling the UK after 15:30. Those calling the United States should start dialing after lunch and because of the time difference, tend to work on a UK campaign before lunch. Generally, however, all agents should work seven hours a day, with an unpaid lunch break of 30 minutes to an hour and 20 minutes paid break, 10 minutes each morning and afternoon.

Given the complications of the particular markets and time zones, let us see how the management monitors what times agents are working and where they are calling.

Monitoring

The management monitors agents electronically, in three key ways: timesheets, statistics, and call outcomes.

Electronic timesheets

Any information, such as the time agents start and finish their workday, the length of their lunch break, which campaigns they work on during a given day, and which country(s) they call is logged manually by agents in their electronic timesheets.

Dial reports and statistics

During their training, agents are told they are expected to make at least 30 dials/hour and between 200 and 250/day. They are shown how to open a company record and press a dial button (Figure 2.2), allowing them

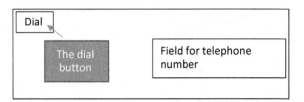

Fig. 2.2   Dialing through the system

to dial the phone number displayed on the screen. This is called "dialing through the system" as opposed to manual dialing that would involve typing each number on the keyboard.

However, agents are not told that whenever they press "dial," there is an electronic record made of the call. This information is collected on a minute-by-minute basis and is available to the management. The screenshot below (Figure 2.3) provides an example of a dial sheet showing how agents dialed on that day. The first agent made only 61 dials but got seven leads. Thus, the agent managed to contact the right person within a particular company on seven occasions and that person agreed to answer all the required questions.

A record is made of every call an agent makes, the length of the conversation, and the phone number. Statistics are checked continuously to discern whether the agents' times on the phone are appropriate. For every call outcome, there is a standard number of minutes an agent should be on the phone. For instance, if they do not manage to get through to anyone, the call should be around 20–30 seconds long, whereas if they manage to reach a required person, calls should be around two to three minutes long minimum. If the "dial report" shows that some calls have lasted less than 5 seconds, they are considered dummy calls. Agents make dummy calls so they show up in the dial report and in the overall stats, but hang up immediately and do not speak to anyone. Any call that is between one and five seconds long will usually be considered a dummy call. Invalid numbers and voicemails are exceptions.

It is almost impossible for call monitors to spot dummy calls unless they are truly only one or two seconds long because voicemails and invalid numbers are logged identically in the system, the only difference being

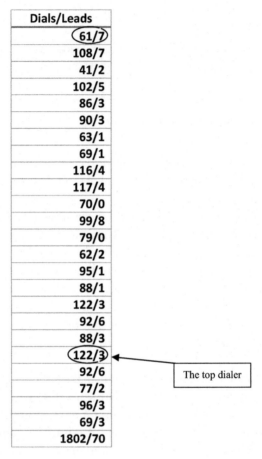

Fig. 2.3 Dial/lead statistics

small differences in call length. Agents may arouse suspicion if they only have very short calls (lasting only a second or two). A call monitor may try to listen in secretly to see what the agent is doing and may spot the agent doing "dummy calls." If an agent claims to have identified a lead but the call lasted less than two minutes, they will be questioned. Although it is not actually the case, agents are led to believe that the corporate management on the floor upstairs also conducts monitoring of the call center downstairs. The floor upstairs is shrouded in mystery for agents and they are unlikely to interact with upstairs management.

Assumptions about how long a call should last are estimated by the length of the script, with the belief that verbatim readings of any script last at least two to three minutes. If agents meet their weekly lead targets, depending on the campaign, they may receive a bonus of around £100 extra per week to incentivize them. If they perform poorly, this will not be reflected in their pay.

Statistics are also often used to indicate whether it is necessary to monitor an individual's calls. With only one call monitor and at peak times almost 80 agents, it is impossible for the call monitor to listen to every agent. But if an abnormality is spotted in the dial report, the call monitor can hone in on that agent. In order to offer support, the management and call monitor need another kind of information that all new agents are taught to produce as part of the systems training: the "call outcomes."

Call outcomes

Every time agents make a call, they are required to log its outcome. The different outcomes are usually derived from the campaign script. The following outcome list is from a hand-out used as a reference during the systems training (Table 2.2).

Logging call outcomes correctly is essential for the call center for two reasons. First, agents can be monitored and supervised. When managers access individual statistics, they look at the duration of a call and the outcome, providing them with an idea of what happened on the phone, what kind of conversation it was, and with whom the agent spoke in the company. In this sense, monitoring is a tool for the management to identify the source of problems, how well agents are working, whether they need coaching, and the quality of their data. Since call outcomes are always logged in English, it is possible to monitor calls and campaigns quickly by country even if the campaign manager or team leader does not understand the language in which the call was conducted. Secondly, all the data accumulated in the dial report is then summarized, analyzed, and sent back to the clients. Clients take this information as an indicator of how the specific product/service/event that agents are pitching is perceived by their target audience. This kind of information, collated for the client, is based on a set of statistics: the "dial report."

Table 2.2 Call outcomes

Call outcome	Definition
Lead	When the contact agrees to all the questions on the script and his/her company matches the campaign criteria for the lead definition they must also agree to speak to the client after our initial call
Bad data	When the company details are incorrect or a duplicate company has been identified
Call back	You should only use this option when you speak to the contact directly. Call is used only when the contact him/herself asks you to call back another time
IT outsourced	When the company does not have an IT Department or anyone else who makes IT decisions. Normally this option is also valid when the company uses an external company to handle their IT
Not contacted	This outcome can be used for all those various reasons when you do not get through to the contact. When a receptionist, colleague, or the PA of the contact asks you to call back that is considered as a Not Contacted, not Call Back
Not interested	This option should only be used when you speak to the correct contact (one of the target audience) and he/she refuses your offer
Screen out	When a company does not match the campaign criteria. (e.g., if employee size is out of range; the contact spoken to is not one of the Target Audience; etc.) Employee size no less than 100+ in UK

In Figure 2.4, the agent did not always save a call outcome after every call, and this is not unusual. However, it becomes clear from the report that in the timeframe recorded the agent spoke only once to a target person; this call is logged as a "call back." The other calls are identifiable as "Not-Contacted-Other" from the length and from the logged call outcome. In this one case, no one picked up the phone from the switchboard, the target contact was on voicemail/out of the office, or the gatekeeper would not put the agent through. What would be apparent for every manager and team leader from this dial report, however, is that even though this is a poor record, all her calls are of the required length. The next step would be for the call monitor to understand from the conversations why she has not made a lead yet, whether it was a data problem, what she says, or just bad luck.

Total Dials:	124
Total Call Duration:	2:10:37
Total Successful Dials:	122
Total Unsuccessful Dials:	2
Average Call Duration:	1:05
Average Call Duration for Contacted Calls:	01:30

No	Call Date	Start Time	End Time	Duration	Phone Number	Country	Dial Status	Call Outcome
1	X	09:47:47	09:47:49	00:00:02	X	UK	Failed	-
2	X	09:47:56	09:48:17	00:00:21	X	UK	Success	-
3	X	09:51:32	09:53:08	00:01:36	X	UK	Success	Not Contacted-Gatekeeper
4	X	09:53:47	09:54:38	00:00:51	X	UK	Success	Call Back
5	X	09:57:03	09:57:35	00:00:32	X	UK	Failed	No Contacted-Other
6	X	09:57:43	09:58:43	00:01:00	X	UK	Success	Not Contacted-Other
7	X	10:00:01	10:00:54	00:00:53	X	UK	Success	-
8	X	10:00:39	10:01:32	00:00:53	X	UK	Success	Not Contacted-Other
9	X	10:02:49	10:04:02	00:01:13	X	UK	Success	Not Contacted
10	X	10:05:17	10:06:24	00:01:07	X	UK	Success	-
11	X	10:10:12	10:13:23	00:01:48	X	UK	Success	Not Contacted
12	X	10:17:44	10:18:58	00:03:11	X	UK	Success	Not Contacted-Other
13	X	10:19:20	10:19:44	00:01:14	X	UK	Success	Not Contacted-Other
14	X	10:20:02	10:20:54	00:00:24	X	UK	Success	-
15	X	10:21:20	10:24:24	00:00:52	X	UK	Success	-

Fig. 2.4   The dial report

Even though the detailed dial report is available to all the managers, it is common for them to rely on a shorter overview of all the statistics (Figure 2.5). This shorter statistical display provides not only an overview of all the agents' results in the call center, but is quicker to access. This tool thus makes it possible to monitor individual agents and their entire campaign performance on a minute-by-minute basis in terms of both numbers of dials and contents. The statistics appear in the following format.

Both the dial report and the overview of the statistics are generated over a browser, as the entire call center software and the backup process is internet-based. Therefore, managers and team leaders need only press the refresh button on their browser in order to update and reload the

Date 10-09-XXXX
Dials/Leads
175/16
141/6
124/0
106/0
149/10
128/2
144/2
170/9
120/7
155/0
120/7
103/08
217/5
156/11
202/4
154/6
54/4
89/2
188/4
150/8
169/10
182/5
TOTAL: 3346/130

Fig. 2.5 Overview of dials and leads per agent 1

overview every minute. Everything is generated and saved on the internet. Because of the sheer mass of data involved it is a slow process to open any kind of statistics from the system. On days when the internet speed (bandwidth) is slow, for instance when the call center operates at full capacity, this takes even longer. Out of all the statistics, the general overview (Figure 2.5) is the quickest, thus the most frequently used by the management and team leaders. On the other hand, it may take almost three minutes to open the individual dial report with all the outcomes for the entire day. Consequently, it is less often accessed by the campaign managers. Nonetheless, team leaders and the call monitor look at both kinds of reports since it is their job to find out whether and why agents are struggling, to help them, and to report back to the campaign manager.

Agents are not left in the dark about how many dials and leads they are making and whether they are on track. This information is available to them in a limited form. During systems training, they are shown how they can check their own and other's statistics in terms of dials and leads. The statistics, however, only provide an overview. Agents cannot access the detailed dial report. The overview provides agents with an idea of whether they have met the daily targets, the leads and dials, expectations outlined on the brief they received.

Systems training

I have already explained some parts of the systems training, such as how to log on (electronic timesheets), how to dial, the need to save a call outcome after every dial and also how to access one's own statistics. The other part of the systems training is about how to process electronically all the information agents obtain over the phone, for there is a particular way information needs to be entered into the call center's database or that of the client. When agents phone companies, they often come across completely new information or discover information that needs to be amended, such as if a contact listed in the database has left the company or is listed incorrectly. For instance, *Silvio Berlusconi* was listed in the Italian database as an IT Manager for a particular firm. This is likely the result of someone playing a joke as this is also the name of a well-known Italian politician. Therefore, the agent who discovered this was required to ask the gatekeeper at the company for the names of the parties responsible for IT. They would add the new names and the email or mailing addresses to the database, and update the valid existing ones. In the brief given to agents, a small section (Figure 2.6) outlines the call center's policy for updating and adding records.

New agents are shown how to create new records during the systems training and how to log the information that a person does not work at a particular company anymore. They are warned not to delete any old information as the logs are cumulative and information can be traced back to the agent who made the changes. It is made clear that no field

---

Adding and updating records:

- Ensure you keep the integrity of the database and update any fields that may require updating (e.g., new address, new contact, etc.)

- When adding new information select a new line NEVER delete old information

---

Fig. 2.6 Adding and updating records

should ever be blank and for every contact, an agent must obtain the first name, surname, job title, email address, and company address of the person accepting the call. According to management, it is important to spend considerable time on training new agents on data entry as they may choose not to update the database if they do not know how, do not understand the value of data entry, or believe it to be too time-consuming, prioritizing their dial rates and lead targets. Agents are more likely to meet their targets with correct data in their database so management works to assure they are aware of this. Yet the constant tension for agents is that data entry and updating the database takes away time from being on the phone meeting high dial rates and lead targets. Although team leaders will have told agents about the importance of data entry, it takes newer agents some time to value correct data and understand how their lack of data entry can affect their colleague's success on the phone as everyone uses the same database to make calls.

Campaign training

On behalf of a variety of different clients, often well-known multinational blue chip companies, the call center offers project-based work to agents to contact IT and decision makers of businesses in countries around the globe for marketing, customer development, and sales purposes. The service the call center offers usually involves the IT or business decision maker agreeing to receive an email offering clients' complimentary reports, webinars, or details about events. If an IT or business decision maker has been identified as interested in a product, answers all the questions on the client-approved script, and agrees to be called back, this is logged as a "lead."

The European countries, Russia, Turkey, South Africa, Saudi Arabia, the Emirates, the United States, and Canada are commonly involved. I know of campaigns that targeted India, China, Hong Kong, Japan, Iran, and Brazil. If there is an enquiry for a certain country and the call center can find a caller that speaks the appropriate language(s), they run it.

The agents contact IT and business decision makers through a variety of call types. One of these is "cold calling," in which the agent contacts organizations randomly from the call center or the clients' database. The call center also uses "warm data," which means that the client provides the call center with a list of companies that may already be customers or have expressed an interest in certain products by registering online or through magazines. This interest is then "nurtured" by the call center through call contacts until the moment when the engagement reaches the sales point and the call is passed to the client.

Most opportunities identified by an agent are at the top of a "sales funnel," a metaphor used to represent a customer's journey from becoming aware of a product (through "marketing" in the early stages) to buying it ("sale"), and thus represent early stages that can potentially lead to a sale for the client. Interest tends to be generated if a person in a targeted company agrees to receive an email about a certain product. The call center also offers "BANT campaigns" and the "nurturing" calls mentioned above both of which are further down the funnel, closer to being converted to a sale, and thus more expensive for the client.

A BANT (budget, authority, need, timeframe) campaign is different from an engagement campaign. The agent calling in a BANT campaign is looking for companies with specific needs that allow a client to sell their products. For a BANT lead, the agent needs to talk to a decision maker who has a budgeted project for which client products are appropriate. The contact needs to be made within a timeframe. The next step is nurturing the lead over a longer period of time by providing trials and exclusive information to maintain customer interest and engage them until they are ready to buy. At that point, the lead is passed back to the client. During campaign training, agents learn the processes that occur behind lead generation, and are provided with a script (Figure 2.7) containing a text/message that the client wants the agents to read verbatim to a targeted person. The message has an introduction to each potential contact, an introduction

> **The Pitch**
>
> The reason for my call today is that BIS has put together a complimentary report on SBP - Safe Browsing Policy. The SBP is the bedrock of any organization's management of employee use of corporate IT systems. This whitepaper is written by an external company that looks at the legal implications of making sure your SBP is solid. By reading this whitepaper you will learn about:
> - Common mistakes and myths when creating a SBP
> - What should be in an SBP
> - Provide practical tips to maximise compliance and minimise risks
> - Explain how to create and enforce an SBP effectively
>
> Other IT personnel have received it and found it to be very useful. Can I send you the whitepaper it is completely complimentary?

Fig. 2.7 An example of a pitch on a script

to the client, and the pitch itself. Very few of the agents have an IT background and a script is needed so they know what to say.

Agents all use the same pitch on a campaign, so it is easy to monitor and assess them in terms of lead and call targets and the agents' respective performances. In fact, agents are ideally "call monitored" to ensure that they ask all the questions outlined in the pitch and provide all the content written on the script.

The final part of training focuses on "objection handling" to equip agents with what the management calls "soft skills" that may be needed as a call progresses. Agents use the tips and tricks to ensure that the conversation ends in their favor, including how to get past the gatekeeper. For instance, agents are advised to use complicated techy words from the script that a gatekeeper might not be familiar with to make their call sound important and eliminate further questions before transferring the caller. Sometimes an agent can impress a gatekeeper by indicating that he or she is calling from London. For every country, there are different strategies and phrases summarized on special hand-outs.

Regulation of non-work activities during working hours

While agents are on the phone, there are times when their work does not take up all their concentration and they can do something else at the same time, such as when they are on hold. In general, the policy in this respect is relaxed. As long as it does not affect their work performance and productivity, agents are free to talk to their peers, read newspapers or books, play with their smartphones, eat, get up to make themselves coffee, or use the restroom.

With almost 60 agents sitting in a small space talking simultaneously, noise is a constant issue and agents sometimes struggle to hear interlocutors. Consequently, they prefer chatting via text or hand-written notes. While agents are allowed to surf the internet on their smartphones at any time, as mentioned, there is no full internet access during working hours on their computers. For example, YouTube is blocked, although agents often find ways around this. Management, unbeknownst to agents, recently introduced software to view agents' screens remotely, but like the dial report, this method is slow. Hence, by the time a suspicious manager finally views an agent's screen the agent is likely to have completed their YouTube viewing.

After their initial training day, agents discover that there is no dress code. It is so uncommon for anyone to wear a suit that if someone wears one, it is assumed that either they have a job interview or they must be new. Many agents take advantage of this policy by cross-dressing, wearing religious themed clothing, or donning items that express their affiliation to a subculture, such as punk. Managers, like agents, choose to dress casually. It can thus be difficult for newcomers to discern who is a manager. This can create confusion as we will see later.

So far the description of the first day of a typical new call center agent has introduced several features of the workplace that, despite call centers' reputations in the literature as standardized, tend to complicate the achievement of uniformity:

(i) flexibility of the work itself such as its project-based nature and dependency on clients' wishes,
(ii) the sheer range of countries called and thus the language(s) required by agents,
(iii) the limited number of seats available,
(iv) the need for spontaneous recruitment to keep up with clients' wishes and agents' departures,
(v) the nature of cold calling including potential volatility in agents' performances and contact rates.

Management tries to minimize or at least control these variables. Table 2.3 summarizes some of the fundamental efforts at standardization.

Despite these efforts to standardize and control some parts of call center work, there are nonetheless alternatives to standardization in which flexibility is condoned and even encouraged. This concerns, for instance, the seating order, the objection-handling session, and the regulation and non-regulation of non-work related activities. Drawing on the trope of a typical new agent on their first day in the call center, this section conveys a picture of what call center work entails, and also of the mix of standardization, unpredictability, and relaxation that appears to characterize CallCentral. Although we have heard of the "management," "team leaders," and "agents," like a typical new agent we still know little about them. The next section focuses more closely on these categories of employees and the relationships between the different levels in the CallCentral hierarchy in anticipation of a discussion of how individuals talk about the tensions described.

Table 2.3 Some aspects of call center work and the organizational means of control

Aspect of call center work	Standardization	Means of control	Reason
Updating the database	Standardized steps of data entry	Software program to view screens Internal software records any changes	The more accurate the database, the higher probability of making leads Lead with correct info sent to the client
Dials/Leads	A set amount of time the agent is supposed to spend according to the call outcome	Dial sheet/Dial report Call monitoring	Makes agent's performance measurable and comparable
Pitch	Pitch the message approved by the client	Call monitoring	Makes statistics accurate
Call outcomes	An accurate call outcome logged for every call made	Dial report	To produce statistics
Work hours	The agent's day should follow a timetable	Timesheet Internal software Dial report	Transient nature of work and campaigns

The management

New agents learn quickly after their first day, so the term *management* can be ambiguous and contradictory. Roles are not clearly assigned and often overlap. This causes constant conflict and tension among the different levels of authority and responsibility in the hierarchy and among individual managers. What agents assume initially is that the management consists only of the people who sit in the management rows: the call center supervisor, four campaign managers, and two quality control (QC) checkers. The two quality control checkers approach agents if any required information is missing from agent's leads so that agents can augment their report before it is sent off to a client. What the new agents are not told, however, is that everyone in the managerial row has the same boss, the operations manager, who is located on the floor above the call center. Nevertheless, agents learn quickly by observing the management row that some managers are more senior and more powerful than others. Seniority in this case means that one has more influence on the general company management upstairs.

After a few days, new agents realize that there is another part of the organization "upstairs" that is closely related to the call center. Most likely on their way to the call center in the morning, they see people in the lift with special electronic passes allowing them to go to the floor above. Moreover, the campaign managers vanish from time to time for meetings for several hours through a back door in the call center and afterwards they may be talking about "what upstairs says."

Another, more direct point of contact may arise if the call center is operating at full capacity and some agents need to sit upstairs because there are no more seats. At that moment, when they go "upstairs" with a team leader in a group, they come to understand the meaning of this notion. They realize that the European headquarters of a multinational corporation is located on the third floor with a very glossy reception that stands in stark contrast to the call center entrance. Most agents do not want to be moved upstairs, preferring to stay in the main call center. They say that they feel unwanted upstairs. Moreover, no one there interacts with them. Instead, they are constantly watched and stared at. Consequently, they cannot do the things they are allowed to do downstairs such as read a newspaper or text and browse the web on their phones while on hold. New agents are also told by their peers that if anyone applies from within the call center for a permanent position "upstairs" they will not be considered simply because they come from downstairs. It would not matter if they have amazing qualifications and experience. If anyone moves "upstairs," which happens very rarely, it would be a manager.

There are three levels of management in the call center. Company managers are located on the third floor which is also the top floor above the team leaders and the active phoning level. Company management is referred to internally as "upstairs." Call center management is "downstairs." This is where the call center is located. Included downstairs are the call center supervisor and campaign managers, the second level of management, and their team leaders, the third level, who manage things on their behalf on the call center floor. Quality control and the floor supervisor are also in this group (see Figure 2.8).

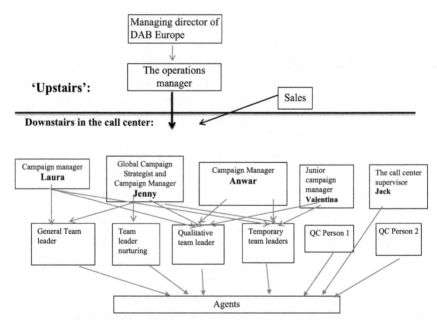

Fig. 2.8 The overall hierarchy

The senior company management: "upstairs"

The call center managers tend to use "upstairs" as a collective term to refer to the senior management of the company. The senior management includes the managing director, the operations manager, and the sales division. Since the call center management downstairs is only a part of the larger company, at 18:00 every day the campaign managers and the call center supervisor go "upstairs" to face senior management. In those meetings they justify the lead results, the statistics, and the performance of every single agent across all campaigns.

The call center management

Jack is the call center supervisor who recruits new agents, carries out initial introductions at agents' training, liaises with the employment agencies for the recruitment of agents, and handles any other human resources matters. The four campaign managers, Valentina, Laura, Jenny, and Anwar, manage around ten campaigns each at any one time in terms of costs, allocating agents to campaigns, and database use. Of them all, Jenny is by far the most senior and powerful. She is influential with those "upstairs" for several reasons.

Unlike other call center managers, Jenny started out as an agent many years ago and worked her way up the hierarchy. Therefore, upstairs believes that she has a good grasp of the call center and its workers. She manages the trickiest situations and campaigns requiring the most expensive nurturing such as those that include customers who are already interested and who deserve special attention in order to generate new sales, and BANT (budget, authority, needs, timeframes) campaigns. BANT campaigns are those that revolve around leads with potentially interested customers who may not only have the authority to agree to a potential sale but also have a need, an approved budget, and timeframe for purchases. Jenny also manages the biggest campaigns in terms of number of agents and lead targets.

The campaign managers' responsibilities are not limited to campaign management; they also coordinate database and network projects with other company-owned call centers around the globe on a daily basis. Perhaps not surprisingly, they are constantly in meetings and do not have much time to deal with agents on the floor. Instead, they delegate the everyday running of campaigns to team leaders.

The management on the floor: the team leaders

A new agent's first contact with a team leader is on their first work day at systems training. Generally there are only two team leaders—the team leader for nurturing campaigns, Stuart, and the team leader for the rest of the campaigns, Ada, but the number of team leaders may vary according to the month of the year as noted above. At peak times, two temporary team leaders may be hired to deal with the campaigns and people. Ada not only does the systems training for new agents, but also handles the campaign training and the debriefs, looks after dials and stats, and more generally liaises between the campaign manager and agents. She is the agent's first point of contact in most matters. Stuart looks after agents working on the high-end nurturing campaigns and sits in the bubble room, having little interaction with the main call center. Let us now look at how the management recruits agents.

Agent recruitment

As mentioned earlier, all agents are hired over the phone on a project basis. In this case, project based means that a blue chip company has asked the call center to generate a specific number of leads per country for their products within a required period of time. Lead targets vary per country depending on the client. The selected target audience can range from a single country to the entire globe. Although CallCentral offers lead generation worldwide, it is common to have smaller lead targets for Asian and Middle Eastern markets, and larger targets for Europe and North America. Blue chip companies generate most of their revenue in Europe and North America, where there is a developed IT infrastructure and about which CallCentral has and owns good databases. Generally, the lead targets for Germany, the UK, and France tend to be the highest overall targets. These "big three" represent the biggest and most lucrative markets. However, the geographical focus of a campaign is determined by the client.

Having a multilingual call center target a wide range of countries in a number of languages is more convenient and cheaper for multinational blue chip companies than having to recruit several call centers. Having one call center instead of several helps clients obtain data that is comparable across different markets. Since most clients want to target many different markets (e.g., Europe, the Middle East, and Asia), some with lead targets as small as 30, an agent speaking a particular language might only be needed for two days with a daily lead target of 15. The call center is continuously in need of different language speakers on a short-term basis. Consequently, the recruitment of speakers of diverse languages is a constant issue. In fact, the country and the language factor significantly impact recruitment, as I explain below.

In a job advertisement used for recruitment online, the call center management distinguishes between work experience (e.g., IT or call center) and language knowledge requirements, with the former being desirable and the latter mandatory. Thus, according to online advertisements for agent positions the only requirement one must fulfill is knowledge of one of a specified set of European languages. The importance of this is visible from the heading "languages" in ads. In spite of the language component of the job, the advertisement does not clarify the level of language proficiency required. That is, the advertisement could be soliciting native, proficient second language speakers, or intermediate speakers. Furthermore the ads fails to specify whether new agents merely need oral skills in a specific language or whether they need to be literate, too. Moreover, although an advertisement suggests that speakers of *all* designated European languages are equally required, new agents realize once they apply or join that hiring and employment practices differ from language to language: certain languages are more in demand and speakers of those languages are paid more.

New agents learn that the demand for language speakers and the work offered depends on a country's degree of technologization—that is, the country's reliance and expenditures on companies that spend significantly on software and hardware—the size of its population, the country's number of official languages, the numbers of speakers of the appropriate languages in London, and the willingness of these speakers to work in a call center. For instance, the UK, France, and Germany are the biggest markets and most populous countries in Europe, so it tends to be comparatively easy to recruit native English, French, and to a lesser extent German speakers. However, the other most targeted regions in Europe, Scandinavia and the Benelux countries, have comparatively small populations and small immigrant communities in London. As a result, the call center always struggles to recruit speakers of Dutch, Flemish, and Scandinavian languages. It is very difficult to find European Dutch speakers, so it is not uncommon to hire the more easily recruited Afrikaans speakers instead as these two languages are mutually intelligible. Often the demand for both Dutch and Scandinavian languages is so high that management makes an announcement to ask whether any agent has friends who speak these languages who might be interested in working at the call center.

With continuously high targets for the Netherlands and the Dutch (Flemish) speaking regions in Belgium, the call center in particular values Dutch (Flemish) speakers. The former tend to be even more highly valued than speakers of Italian and Spanish since when it comes to the IT market, these countries are not as developed or lucrative as Scandinavia, Benelux, or the "big three." Moreover, with significant immigrant Spanish and Italian speaking populations in London, it is easy to find agents for smaller targets and campaigns in these countries. In fact, Spanish and Italian callers earn a few pounds less per hour than Dutch callers or Scandinavian language callers.

Switzerland is the other country that tends to be targeted a lot by the call center in addition to the big three, Benelux, and Scandinavia. The fact that Switzerland and Belgium are both officially multilingual complicates the calling and recruitment process. Ideally, an agent is found who speaks all the languages required per country, but this is rare.

The call center uses two strategies to solve the constant recruitment issue for specific languages. The first is to recruit through a language agency, and the second involves tapping employees with multiple language fluencies. Language agencies provide over 70 per cent of CallCentral's agent-level employees. In such cases, the call center has to pay £15 an hour on top of the standard wage to employ the agent, making such hires costly affairs. This has implications for other agents on the same campaign: the budget will be tighter as a result, putting more pressure on them to hit the lead and dial target goals. At the same time, the call center constantly needs foreign language speakers at short notice, making the use of language agencies convenient. Although language agencies claim to assess applicant's written and spoken language capabilities prior to sending them to the call center, too frequently they send untested applicants just for the money. The benefits and drawbacks of direct recruitment versus relying on an agency is summarized below in Table 2.4.

Since agency callers are expensive, they are the first to be put on hold if there is insufficient work unless they perform exceptionally well. The call center can employ the agent directly only after the agent has worked

Table 2.4 Advantages and disadvantages of direct vs. agency recruitment

Direct recruitment		Recruitment through an agency	
Advantages	Disadvantages	Advantages	Disadvantages
Lower cost	Difficulty to assess language speakers abilities	"Tested and qualified" language speakers	Expensive (an extra 15 pounds an hour per agent)
Less pressure on campaigns because of lower costs	Little commitment from direct agents (not hired through an language recruitment agency)	Constant supply of different kinds of language speakers short term and short notice	Hiring expensive agents through an agency may affect the campaign budget and targets. With many agents from agencies, the overall budget is more constrained with more pressure and less leeway on all agents to hit targets
	With nature of projects, difficult to attract (minority) language speakers short term on a short notice	New agents from agencies more committed and reliable	

at the call center through the language agency for three months. After three months, an agent may continue working at the call center by signing a contract with CallCentral directly ("direct agent") rather going through the language agency. Working directly for the call center means they earn a few pounds more per hour since no money is deducted anymore to pay the language recruitment agency.

The second strategy the call center uses to address the shortage issue and the expense of language agencies is to draw on the expertise of semi-multilingual/semi- fluent speakers as opposed to fluent speakers. They can be assigned to call with a given script translated into different languages. Managers know that translated scripts can reduce the need for fluent or native speakers and can reduce recruitment costs. Of the different kinds of campaigns, engagement campaigns tend to be the most standardized and script based. Leads for those campaigns only have to agree to receive an email and no additional questions need to be answered. Conversely, on high-end campaigns, agents are expected by upstairs and downstairs to have in-depth technical conversations, improvise, and talk "off the script" with clients, expecting high quality leads. Occasionally exceptions are made and semi-fluent speakers are used if the call center cannot find speakers with native fluency, but the client cannot know of this as they are promised "native speakers."

Most agents hired directly are recruited as "native speakers." Anyone is considered "native" who has lived in a country where the target language is spoken or who has a passport from there. Managers will know from an agent's CV if they have beginner or intermediate knowledge of other language(s). If the opportunity arises and there is a shortage of speakers, new agents may then be asked to make calls in other languages they speak as "semi-fluent" speakers using a translated script. Agents are often happy to do this, seeing it as an opportunity to improve their linguistic skills, gain linguistic capital, and become highly valued by the call center. The call center benefits from this arrangement in that they do not have to pay agents the multilingual bonus as they were not recruited as fully multilingual speakers. Nevertheless, agents told me that recruiters outside the call center industry subsequently consider them "native" if they have worked in the required language in a call center (for a more detailed discussion of recruitment practices see Woydack 2016).

Translation potentials of semi-fluent speakers can reduce the number of fully competent speakers of minority languages needed. A script serves as a critical document in these cases, giving agents the foundation for articulating a campaign message in one of several languages for their calls. The script is vital for all agents, although it may be more open to interpretation and revision by agents who are truly fluent in one or more of the languages at issue.

In the following section, I build on the excerpts from interviews with agents to probe how agents talk about their call center experience and why they are working there.

Agent views

Many of my interviewees come from countries outside Britain or have migration backgrounds. I divided them into three types of agents: new, current, and former agents. New agents have been at the call center less than three weeks. Current agents have been there longer than three weeks. Former agents no longer work at the call center.

Of the 60 interviews I conducted, 40 were with current and new agents. With an average capacity of 60 seats at the call center, the sample of my interviewees can be considered representative. Over 20 of the current/new agents I interviewed had left the call center within six months of the interview. Most of the agents were in their twenties and had received some form of higher education (see Table 5.1) although CallCentral makes no mention of educational qualifications as part of the recruitment or on the job advertisement. In fact, it is not uncommon for agents to work at CallCentral after having recently completed an undergraduate or, more likely, postgraduate degree in one of London's 70 universities or higher education colleges.

Agents' rationales for call center work

During interviews, a common answer to why agents had chosen to work at the call center was that the position represented their first job opportunity in London.

Extract 2.1

...the first job that I came across when I was in London was a charity call center job. And then I did that for a while, then left, then went into hardcore telesales. Left that because it was a bit too high pressure, because I was doing other stuff outside of work. And then, I ended up getting a call from an agency, and they said there's a place at [CallCentral]; walked in the front door, and the rest, as they say, is history. (*Stuart, team leader*)

Some of my interviewees said that they moved to London to improve their English. Once in London, they were looking for their first professional experience in a foreign country. Their best chance to get a job was one that allowed them to use their native language.

Extract 2.2

I started working in a call center because I came to London and I didn't speak English properly so I was looking for a job that allowed me to speak Italian. (*Claudia, former team leader*)

Extract 2.3

Well actually I was looking... to get any job where I can speak Finnish at first, and I, I just gave it a shot. (*Piia, former team leader*)

Another agent proposes that the call center represents the first step in the trajectory of "London socialization."

Extract 2.4

Let's say you are from Spain, you come here and your English is maybe not good enough.... You need to improve your language skills.... Well then you can always call Spain.... (*Linda, current agent*) (Adapted from Woydack 2016)

When foreigners come to London they are beginners in several respects. Their proficiency in English is likely low, they might not know their way around the city, and their non-UK-based education and any previous professional experiences might not be valued. Their only skill likely to be accredited in the job market at that moment is their expertise in a foreign language as a native speaker. In this sense, the call center can represent the first step in their local integration.

Linda considers the call center job to be temporary. It mainly functions as an introduction to life in London and a source of income. For Stuart, the call center work is in the first part of his day which allows him to devote the rest of the day to pursuing his dream of acting and television. Roberto's story appears to echo Linda's notion of call centers and Londoner socialization.

Extract 2.5

…the reason why I work in this call center, because when I moved to London my first idea was to, just improve my English and then try to find a more qualified job. (…) To be honest, the first thing that I managed to get was a job in a call center, so this is why, and that's why I'm still, I'm still working in here. (*Roberto, current agent*)

Later in the interview, Roberto acknowledged that as a result of the call center experience he "learned how to improve my listening in English with English accent speakers." Tina and Miguel also mention the theme of learning as an incentive to join the call center.

Extract 2.6

(…) at that time I'm looking for a job and the economic crisis just started and I can't find any other better jobs, but I think call center might be a good opportunity for me to practice my English and get some money, so that's why (…). (*Tina, former agent*)

Extract 2.7

> One of the greatest things about this job is that it gave me the opportunity to call in English as well, and I know that my first calls weren't so good as they are now, for example. I really think that in the month and a half I improve a lot in English. Now I feel a lot more confident when I call in English. And that's really good, that's really, really good; it's like to take a course in which you are being paid instead of paying. (*Miguel, current agent*) (Adapted from Woydack 2016)

According to my observations, scripts are also crucial in enabling callers with little proficiency in English to communicate adequately in this language. Agents who are beginners or intermediate speakers of languages always ask for a translated script before they call and find the standardized scripts helpful.

Extract 2.8

> Well, I used a lot of these scripts for one reason and one reason only because, when I started, obviously my level of English was so low.... (*Claudia, former team leader*) (Source: Woydack and Rampton 2016)

Extract 2.9

> It [the script] has been very helpful, especially for me who doesn't... I mean I understand a lot of German but I can't get the main grammar perfect. I'm very communicative, but... make loads of mistakes and people are laughing at the end of the line but, the message is going through and I think the script has been very helpful for me. (*Linnea, current agent*) (Adapted from Woydack 2016)

As Claudia and Linnea indicate, the script provides the agents with a foundation upon which they can base their speech. Joining the call center to develop one's language skills thus represents an important motive for agents.

The interviewees also emphasize the benefit of the temporary, non-committed nature of the job. This allows agents to look for other jobs or to study while earning money.

Extract 2.10

To be honest: I needed the money. I had another job eight weeks ago but the company went into administration. Most of the time people only stay there for a few months as they are looking for another job. (*Vanessa, current agent*)

Extract 2.11

... I enjoy working here much better than I have at other places... it makes a big difference since obviously most of us are trying for other careers. (*Michael, new agent*)

The short-term nature of the job allows flexibility:

Extract 2.12

I was grateful that I had somewhere that would allow me to be flexible at first because, you know, I was kind of in the process of starting my own business and it allowed me to work three days a week. (*Ian, current agent*)

Extract 2.13

The 9–5 thing is very good for me so... after five o'clock I don't think about the job, I just go and do my own thing. (*Rabeya, current agent*)

Rabeya and Ian, as with Stuart, pursue call center work mainly to earn money, whereas the rest of their time is dedicated to their other interests such as university and setting up their own business.

Agents earn a few pounds more per hour than the minimum wage and more than they might earn in retail or hospitality. If they meet their weekly targets, they qualify for incentives which amount to £100 or more per week. In spite of that, all my informants agreed that this work is only temporary and emphasized that they did not want to do it for a long time. Nevertheless, their ideas of call center work with respect to their long-term plans differed. Linda's notion of London socialization suggests that she believes that an individual's stay at the call center is going to be very short. She does not specify a time period required for the socialization; some agents manage to feel they have acquired a new level of socialization within a few weeks, and others may take months. Equally, Vanessa and Tina see this job as a springboard to something better. Although Rabeya, Ian, and Stuart think the same way, their view of call center work is perhaps a bit more long term as their career objectives cannot be realized as quickly as those of other agents (Figure 2.9).

Agents' perceptions of a call center job include the assessment that it is not only easy to obtain, but does not require long-term commitment. The call center job is a position where little if any previous knowledge is required, but it still allows the applicant to "learn" and improve their skills, thanks largely to the script. Universally, the call center represented for agents a transitional moment in their lives and it was a means to an end.

Agents' experience of the call center

Agents' comments about their experiences are mixed. Several newer agents such as Tom, Jonas, and Michael explained that considering the awful reputation of call centers, they were positively surprised.

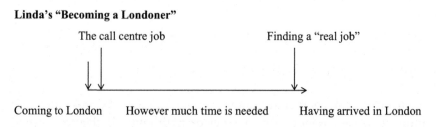

Fig. 2.9 Linda's "Becoming a Londoner"

Extract 2.14

When I got the job I googled like call center and like all these forums warned better don't do it [for] all these reasons. People complaining and I thought based on the work I made the worst choice in my life. But the good thing is that we are not selling anything and I think that's crucial.... you feel like you don't have that much pressure. (*Tom, new agent*)

Extract 2.15

I am positively surprised because in Germany call center work has a very bad reputation. It's very pleasant and one is not put under too much pressure. (*Jonas, new agent*)

Extract 2.16

There's a taboo with call centers you know because it's stigmatized and it's not on the same level as a traffic warden or anything like that. (*Tom, new agent*)

Extract 2.17

We have it pretty relaxed here.... They [agents] get along pretty well considering this mixed nationalities and everything. (*David, current agent*)

Extract 2.18

There are definitely worse jobs out there and seen as a social term, I'm not complaining (...). Here, I think they do it quite well. (*Tom, new agent*)

Agents are largely appreciative of the personal space they are allowed, enabling them to work on good social, informal, and flexible terms. But some agents also complained about the lack of individuality allowed. This was expressed in terms of (i) the relationship between managers and agents and (ii) the overtly inflexible nature of targets. There are critical accounts about the professional relationships between managers and agents. In fact, agents Linda, Andreas, and Barbara complain specifically about the treatment they received from the managers in the call center.

Extract 2.19

> It's the attitude that the managers have to us workers that is a really important thing because sometimes I feel it is a little bit like big fish in a small pond syndrome like sometimes I feel like I'm back to a school class and I'm like when did this happen. (…) You don't feel respected there. I'm sure it's because most people there are like those who work there, the callers inevitably they don't respect it either. It's just a work you do for money really to pay your bills. You don't put an effort into it. (*Linda, current agent*)

Linda connects the lack of respect from the managers to agents' professional indifference. Marta shares Linda's concern and suggests that the loss of individuality may be a universal characteristic of call centers.

Extract 2.20

> It might be it is just general things not only about call centers, but I think you are treated like chickens, you are on a chicken farm, and I think a bit more individual approach, if possible, because [the] well-being of your workers is very important. (*Marta, former agent*)

Andreas has a similar view.

Extract 2.21

> … I felt like a chicken in a cage and somebody stands behind you and waits with a whip and and you know (…) it's really tough and that stresses you out. (*Andreas, former agent*)

Extract 2.22

> It's a bit like a human factory or a human prison I think (…) You are not in a cell but you're strapped to a desk and a computer and a target list of calls. (*Stuart, team leader*)

Tina said the following about the atmosphere.

Extract 2.23

Well, the atmosphere I would say when I first went in, the manager was very relaxed and I don't think there was too... much pressure there, but I heard people complaining about the pressure, the targets and so on. Well, maybe different people perceive in different ways. (...) I made friends in the call center, and yeah, actually it's a very relaxed environment. (*Tina, former agent*)

Many comment on their continuous struggle with targets. Eight informants evoked the imagery of the human vs. machine to capture this fight on the phone. Remarkably enough, not a single interviewee complained about the existence of scripts. Miguel summarizes this constant struggle and contradiction for agents working in a standardized environment rather poignantly:

Extract 2.24

An outbound call center needs the people because they have this human skill that sometimes accomplish[es tasks] like going through a gatekeeper, for example. But the ironic thing is that, at the same time, the longer you spend in a call center, the less human skills you can show at work because your tone of voice sooner or later start[s] to get a bit more monotonous maybe. (*Miguel, current agent*)

Miguel and David lament that all targets and numbers set by the management are the same across campaigns and do not take into account either humans or the unpredictability factor.

Extract 2.25

Of course, you have your off days, and those days you... I think you are like fighting an already lost fight which is fighting against, for example, your target which is for people making enough calls, because you cannot cheat that system; you are trying to fight a number. And if you're trying to fight emotions I guess, [by] numbers, you're going to lose. And, again, that's your off days, your bad days. I think that in the long term you discover that even your managers know that we are human beings; we cannot always perform in the same way, but sometimes when you're calling you forget that and you want to perform always as your best day. (*Miguel, current agent*)

Extract 2.26

> To give them a target and to be punished for not reaching that target when it's out of their hands, I think it's a bit harsh. (*David, current agent*)

Claudia found that this constant pressure burned out agents. From her experience, "there is a moment in which you say, yeah, look I can't touch the phone, or I am not going to reach these targets anymore."

In summary, my interviewees taken together have an ambivalent experience of the call center. On the one hand, they appreciate the social terms and the personal freedoms they enjoy while working; on the other hand, they are critical of the sometimes unrealistic demands placed on them. On the whole, they try to make the most of their time there, for instance, by improving their language skills. In any case, all my interviewees thought that they would stay at the call center for only a short time, that is, less than six months. And in fact, by the time I had completed this research project, none of the agents I interviewed still worked at CallCentral.

Conclusion: the significance of the script at CallCentral

To this point I have explored the organization and functioning of CallCentral, discussing the internal hierarchy, connections with clients, and targets and goals for campaigns. I highlighted the everyday practices of call agents in the process of their work and have drawn attention to the script as underpinning many aspects of a call center's operation. The script is a means for management to maintain control and to standardize and measure some aspects of the work, including agents' performances. Their performances should be calculable, controllable, predictable, and efficient for the management in the face of many unpredictable factors such as the nature of cold calling and the project-based nature of the work. Without standardized scripts, it would be impossible to gather statistics or to monitor agents' performance (see section on "call outcomes"). Without a script, many would find it impossible to work in the call center, either because they lack IT knowledge or because their language skills are insufficient. The script can thus be imagined as a spider whose web covers various phases of CallCentral's work (Figure 2.10).

The question of why agents are critical of targets but not of scripts has emerged in this opening discussion. Moreover, why do agents consider the call center a relaxed place (e.g., Extracts 2.13 and 2.23) but also stressful and inflexible (e.g. Extracts 2.20 and 2.21)? The induction of a new agent and the work of making calls from the point of view of an agent is too narrow a perspective to fully understand the organization and its

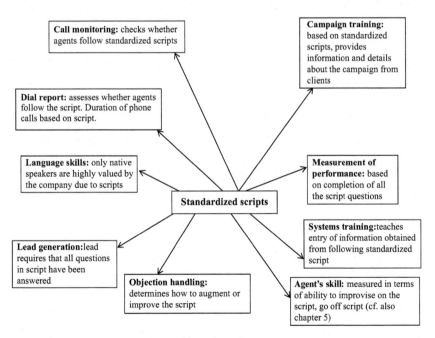

Call monitoring: checks whether agents follow standardized scripts

Campaign training: based on standardized scripts, provides information and details about the campaign from clients

Dial report: assesses whether agents follow the script. Duration of phone calls based on script.

Language skills: only native speakers are highly valued by the company due to scripts

Standardized scripts

Measurement of performance: based on completion of all the script questions

Systems training: teaches entry of information obtained from following standardized script

Lead generation: lead requires that all questions in script have been answered

Objection handling: determines how to augment or improve the script

Agent's skill: measured in terms of ability to improvise on the script, go off script (cf. also chapter 5)

Fig. 2.10 The script and its relation to different aspects of call center work

tensions, or the misfits among managers,' team leaders,' and agents' perceptions of standardization. Thus, in view of the script's centrality for the organization, in the next three chapters I follow "the career of a script" to understand and examine these contradictions, tensions, and the way standardization practices actually play out.

References

Woydack, Johanna. 2016. Superdiversity and a London Multilingual Call Centre. In *Engaging Superdiversity: Recombining Spaces, Times and Language Practices*, ed. Karel Arnaut, Martha Sif Karrebaek, Massimiliano Spotti, and Jan Blommaert, vol. 7, 220–251. Bristol: Multilingual Matters.

Woydack, Johanna, and Ben Rampton. 2016. Text Trajectories in a Multilingual Call Centre: The Linguistic Ethnography of a Calling Script. *Language in Society* 45 (05): 709–732.

3

The First Stage of the Script's Career: Production of the Master Script

Introduction

This chapter is about the first stage of the script's career, which begins when a client contacts the call center about a campaign they would like to run. I address the following questions: By what processes is a script entextualized for a client campaign? What information is prioritized during various meetings to design the script and for what reasons? What are the orientations of management and client toward the script?

First, it is useful to develop a campaign that will set the career of a script in motion. In what follows, I introduce an anonymized model campaign to create a pretext for the production, adaptation, and enactment of the script described in this and the next two chapters (see Figure 3.1). I present a model campaign to underpin the discussion of the script's career and to allow me to explain the details of the contractual expectations at the level of the "the institutional system." The second part of the chapter focuses on the "production of a script" (Figure 3.4).

For our model campaign, an IT blue chip company I call "Best Internet Security" (BIS) has contacted the call center. In the table below

© The Author(s) 2019
J. Woydack, *Linguistic Ethnography of a Multilingual Call Center:*
London Calling, Communicating in Professions and Organizations,
https://doi.org/10.1007/978-3-319-93323-8_3

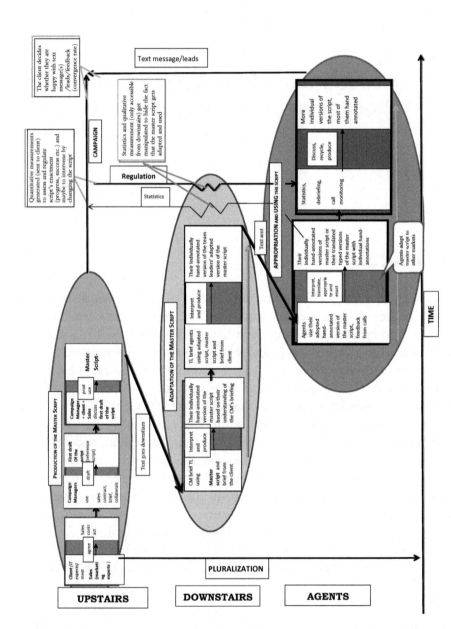

Fig. 3.1 The entire career of the script

Table 3.1 Details of the model campaign

Client name	Best Internet Security (BIS)
Target for the campaign	4,000 engagement leads in total across the UK, France, Germany [engagement leads = information on company and contact details]
Size of companies to be targeted	50–1,000 employees
Industries to be targeted	All
Target audience	All IT professionals
Timeframe	1 month but with weekly delivery of engagement leads
Possible Collaterals [items the client wants the call center to send to the targets]	These should be emailed to the targeted audience (all IT professionals): 1 e-book on best practices for IT security 1 report on IT compliance 1 whitepaper/ report (SBP—Safe Browsing Policy) to be the basis of the agent's script

Adapted from Woydack and Rampton (2016)

(see Table 3.1) I outline the kind of engagement campaign they would like to run. This would be written on their sales brief.

This is an anonymized campaign closely modeled on a real one. I have also anonymized the campaign's master script as described below.

What happens when the client BIS (Best Internet Security) contacts the call center about a campaign they would like to run? Since script productions occur mostly away from the call center, I had little opportunity to observe this stage myself. Hence, for the description of this process I draw on interviews with three campaign managers downstairs who play a key part in this phase. The discussion here is based primarily on employee reports, unlike discussions in subsequent chapters that involve participant observation.

The three campaign managers I interviewed are:

- *Jenny*—Senior Campaign Manager, responsible for all the call centers belonging to CallCentral worldwide. As part of her role she is often involved in the sales meetings that are focal topics in this chapter.
- *Laura*—Senior Campaign Manager for London.
- *Anwar*—Senior Campaign Manager for London.

On the whole, Jenny's account focused on the overall aims of the script production from a commercial point of view and for the corporation.

Conversely, Laura and Anwar talked more about the practical issues and concerns that arise when drafting scripts. In spite of their differing points of view and experiences, all three describe the production of a script as a lengthy process that involves a lot of discussions and meetings, during which new texts are produced to form the basis of *the* master script.

Features of the institutional system: contractual expectations

All three campaign managers stressed that from the perspective of the company management upstairs, the script is a particular product sold to the client. In the eyes of both the corporate management and the client, once a script is paid for the document is ready for implementation without further adjustments. The upstairs managers accept their clients' right to transparency and accountability and have created feedback mechanisms through monitoring and data logging to insure these. The script itself becomes an important means to convey and achieve transparency and accountability.

As a result, as part of the contract with a client, three elements are agreed upon to enable the client to influence the script's production and its later use.

First, the script has to be based on "collaterals"—a collection of media such as an e-book, a report, a whitepaper, or a software trial. These are used to support a sale or service chosen by the client to be passed on to their targeted audience for this campaign. Anwar explains:

Extract 3.1

> The conventional method [for the campaign manager before starting the first draft of the script] is to wait to receive assets (whitepapers, etc.) from the client. That tells us what the topic [of the script and the campaign more generally] is about and what can be written about it [within the script]. (*Anwar, campaign manager*)

In the case of the BIS campaign, the whitepaper/report to be sent out is about Safe Browsing Policy SBP which means that the master script for this campaign should also be on this subject. Apart from the "assets," as

Laura says, the other source for the production of the script is a specific "call to action" from the client:

Extract 3.2

> [When we draft the script] we need to go through a call to action that we need to present from the client. *(Laura, campaign manager)*

Laura uses the marketing phrase *call to action*, which is a specific message to be delivered by an agent to convince the person contacted to accept an email containing the attachments (the client's assets) and to open them. In marketing, prompting people to do something (e.g., click on something) through the use of texts and graphics (e.g., an email or script) is referred to as a *call to action*, a set of measurable objectives inscribed in the contract that the campaign is supposed to achieve. In the call center case, clients also attach to their call to action a corresponding call-to-action-email to be sent out by the agent after every "successful call." The text of this email will have been composed by the client and cannot be amended by either upstairs or the campaign manager.

Second, the contract states that the client is not the only party involved in the script production, but is the party to have the last say. Regarding this, Laura states:

Extract 3.3

> Yeah, you need to send it [script] to the client and if they're not happy you need to amend or change your ad or image, yeah. *(Laura, campaign manager)*

The **third** element is that the management upstairs provides assurance to the client that agents will follow the script word for word without individual variation, to ensure consistency across phone calls. This is written into the contract. Although I do not have a copy of an actual contract, promotional brochures promise clients that they will be consulted and advised on any script changes. Responses from interviewees, and my field notes, suggest that the assurance to clients that agents will follow a script word for word really matters. In a similar vein, Johnstone (2003, 273) points out that a call center's reputation and its capacity to attract clients can rest on its guarantee that individuals follow the script word for word without individual variation. In fact, a client's belief that agents follow a pre-written, approved script word for word has also been a frequent focus for the literature on call centers and is considered a well-known industry fact (e.g., Johnstone 2003, 273; Farrell 2009, 190). Cameron (2000b, 324), for instance, has argued that the process of branding has been extended to the verbal behavior of employees and scripts are instrumental in this. CallCentral's publicity brochure from upstairs advertises the call center's "cost effective" services. The client is assured that "clients will be consulted and advised on script changes." My understanding is that this refers to any changes in the wording of the final script previously approved by the client, and the assumption seems to be that unless communicated otherwise, agents will follow the approved script word for word.

Stuart, one of the more experienced team leaders who has participated in script production meetings and has talked with clients, confirmed this when he told me:

Extract 3.4

The client always gets final send-off [on the script]. And, as far as the client's aware, that is what is said. (*Stuart, senior team leader*)

As Anwar (Extract 3.5) told me during an interview, "getting the correct message across" (the client's message) is central for the client. Additionally, as Field note entry 3.1 below shows, for the client the scripts are a means of carrying out marketing and branding, and providing a follow-up customer service to existing or potential new customers.

Extract 3.5

JW: Why do you use scripts?

A: This again is to keep consistency in the message being delivered to the targeted audience by different agents who are working on the same project. (…) Quality of work is essential and we need to make sure that the correct message is reaching the targeted audience. (*Anwar, senior campaign manager*)

In an environment where the client places a premium on textual fidelity and also pays for it, following the script becomes an indicator and a benchmark for delivering good quality, as Anwar's (Extract 3.5) and Jenny's comments (Extract 3.6), and the vignette (Field note entry 3.1) below illustrate.

Extract 3.6

We prefer people read from the scripts (…) and that regulates what everyone's saying across the calls. (*Jenny, campaign manager*)

Field Note Entry 3.1 Delivering textual fidelity to please a new high-profile client X

Sales had finally managed to sign client X, one of the biggest and most important clients in IT after having failed to sign them for years. After the sales had been agreed, Jenny told me in the panic room that this campaign had to be top-notch quality. She (and upstairs) wanted to impress client X. Thus, she had not only arranged for the best agents to work on this campaign but it was my job to ensure that agents follow client X's script word for word. As she put it, working for this client is a dream come true. So if any agents did not follow the script, I should let her know and she would make sure they did. Moreover, according to her, this campaign is not about smashing the daily targets (quantity), but about delivering quality. In this case quality means following client X's script.

Stuart further notes that the client's influence is so strong during the phase of the script's production that the script becomes "artificial." For him, the script has been put together by "corporate people," that is, the client. I also read into his statement that he is pointing out the irony within the script's production and the later proceedings, which are often remarked upon by the campaign managers. On one hand, the client signs a contract with the idealized notion of imposing a specific script on agents, but then it relies on a call center full of human beings to spread the message and make it more personal. After all, the client could spread the "message" to the targeted audience via email, a service which the call center also offers, but they do not do that; most likely, people would delete it unread. So the client wants a personal touch, but in a sense they do not. However, the client ultimately knows that they need human beings in the call center to get past the gatekeeper at their selected customer organizations so the message can actually be delivered to the target audience. Stuart seems to use "corporate" in a derogatory sense, denoting someone distant from real-

ity, someone ignorant of how things at the bottom in the call center actually work. In his eyes artificiality is the end result.

Extract 3.7

> It [the script] is put together by corporate people. It's put together by the
> client who sees it and thinks, "That's exactly the message that this company
> wants to get across," and it seems to me like they completely forget that this
> is human beings talking to human beings. And if someone's going to take a
> report from you or an email or a webinar or whatever it's going to be, it's a
> human dealing with another human being and if you make that artificial
> then in some ways you're negating the point of having a call center. (…)
> They [the client] always get the final send-off, which is why it [the script]
> can sound quite artificial because we're writing to please them, if you know
> what I mean. So they'll go "oh that's exactly the script we want" (…) I mean
> I would make it [script] less formal, but then you have a problem there
> because that won't meet the client's demands. (*Stuart, senior team leader*)

Stuart respects the clients' wishes but seems to imply that the client
may not necessarily know what is best for them and that their (implau-
sible) demands may be more of a hindrance than a help.

There are three sets of statistics that aim to safeguard agents' verbatim
readings, and more importantly, these statistics are meant to allow a client
to regulate and influence proceedings even after the contract has been
signed. Clients are emailed sets of statistics on a weekly basis, enabling
them to monitor the progress of their campaign and the success of their
master script. They can intervene if they feel the need for any changes in the
wording of the master script, as they have the last say on the master script.

The first set of statistics are convergence rates. These are a range of
formulas used to calculate the success of the composition of a script based
on the statistics and the actions (opened the email told about, opened the
attachment, etc.) of the people who were sent the email. As Jenny notes

Extract 3.8

> It's [production of statistics] actually that you can show their convergence
> and their acquisition rate. (*Jenny, senior campaign manager*)

Thanks to advances in technology it is now possible to record, for instance, who clicks on the assets or opens an email. This makes it possible to measure the success of a script and a call to action through a range of mathematical formulas that allow the generation of statistics. Based on these statistics, the client makes a decision as to whether it is necessary to change the wording of the master script. At the same time, all these calculations are based on the assumption that agents follow the script word for word without variation. Clients and upstairs management believe that any variation in the text on the part of the individual agent makes responses noncomparable and this would make it impossible to assess the strength, weakness, or success of the script.

The formulas that are employed for generating statistics use information such as:

- Out of all the calls agents made using the script approved by the client, how many resulted in agents sending out the emails containing the collaterals?
- Out of all the emails sent out, how many of these emails were opened (but not the attachment)?
- Out of the people who were sent emails, how many opened the attachments?
- How many people followed up or used the services provided or advertised as part of the attachments?

These formulas calculate different kinds of "convergence rates." The CallCentral corporate website advertises high rates based on "objective and proven formulas." Of the different scenarios for convergence rate calculations, clients care most about the last one. In the example of the BIS campaign, the client would be interested in calculating the convergence rate for how many people opened the SBP email, how many read it, and how many clicked on the BIS website hot key provided in the email as part of the follow-up engagement.

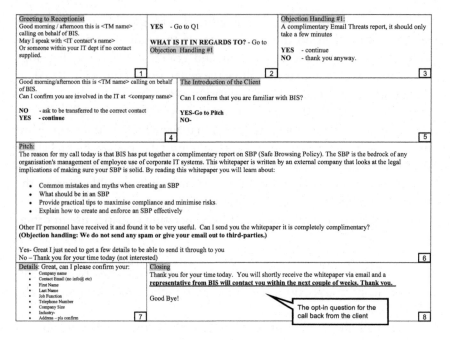

Fig. 3.2 The closing section of the master script. (Source: Woydack 2016)

Sending a client a weekly list of "successful calls" made that week is the second statistical priority. For the call to action to have been successful, the people who have been phoned (the "leads") must have agreed to the opt-in section of the script that asks them if their contact details can be passed on to the client for a follow-up call. As part of any subsequent follow-up call, the client may then ask the contact/lead about the script and the assets that the agent is supposed to have talked to them about (Figure 3.2).

If the contact cannot remember the call with the agent, the name of the client's company, or anything from the script, the client will reject the lead on the assumption that the agent did not follow the script. Often, the rejection is also accompanied by a threat to the call center to pull the campaign. The vignette (Field note entry 3.2) is an example of such an incident where a client was not happy with the feedback they had received from following up the list of contacts (leads) from the call center.

Field Note Entry 3.2 A client complains about lack of quality
During the day, I received several messages on the YIM (Yahoo Instant Messenger) from Jenny telling me that I needed to talk with an agent called Jonas. Jenny told me that a big client had rejected almost all of his leads as they could not remember anything from the script nor about the email containing the assets. Furthermore, the client threatened to pull the campaign if this was not investigated and quality was not improved. She sent me a message on Yahoo Instant Messenger whether I thought the call agent was cheating and what was going on there. My reply was that as far as I was aware he wasn't. The truth was that I always had kept an eye on him not entirely trusting him since I knew that he was very economical with the content of the script (he often left out large chunks). But at the same time he was funny and charismatic on the phone so I had always supposed he would make an impression on people and they would remember the phone calls. However, Jenny also complained that the length of his phone calls was not sufficient. So I took Jonas to the panic room and told him that there had been a serious complaint from the client. I informed him they had threatened to pull the campaign as they are not happy with its quality and I pleaded with him to actually follow the script for this campaign.

The third measure is another specific set of generated statistics, the "dial report" and "dial sheet." Part of the client's contract with CallCentral stipulates that they be delivered on a weekly basis. I introduced these statistical reports in Chapter 2, where I explained that they record how many dials agents make, the outcome of all calls, and their length. Summaries of these are required for the calculation of the convergence rate statistics, so they are a separate set of statistics and a separate information source. That is, while convergence statistics are based on whether people click on the email and open the attachment, the dial report and dial sheet focus on agents' performances and their calls. However, it is important to state that the call-based statistics only rely on quantitative numbers and predictions; qualitative phone monitoring is only done downstairs and is not shared with the client.

Figure 3.3 shows step by step how the production of statistics enables a client to influence the production of the script and its use. In step 1, the client approves a script. Based on that script, in step 2 campaign managers anticipate call length based on the time it takes to read the approved script verbatim, and they predict the number of leads an agent can achieve

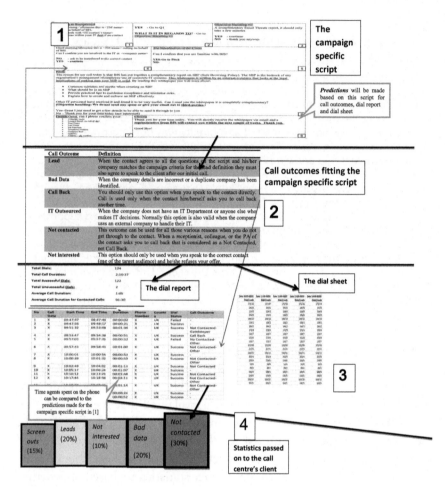

Fig. 3.3 The generation of statistics based on the master script

per diem and the possible call outcomes. When agents implement the script in their calling, they should log every call using the anticipated outcomes so that the dial report statistics can be generated. Thanks to the dial report (step 3) and the dial sheet, the call center management, on behalf of the client, can monitor agents' performances and their productivity by comparing the values originally anticipated with the actual statistics that the computer system records.

For example, if it takes an estimated three minutes to read a client's script but a call logged as successful lasts only one minute, mid-level managers assume the agent could not have followed the script word for word. The dial report in such a case is not shared with the client or with upstairs, but it allows downstairs management to check whether agents are following the script, and it may lead to discussions with agents. In the final step (step 4), instead of sending a client hundreds of long lists of the dial sheets and reports as they are generated every day, data are summarized and analyzed by campaign managers in the form of bar charts for clients. From time to time, these summaries prompt the client to ask for redrafts of the approved script, because they are not happy with the progress of the campaign or the results achieved so far. When a campaign does not go well, upstairs management and clients themselves believe that the call center's clients should be able to influence future happenings and internal proceedings. Their demands should be at the center of the campaign process all the way through.

This institutional system allows a client to influence a script's production and implementation through contractual guarantees. When it comes to the production of the script, the client has a strong influence over wording and content, and has the last say on its form. Moreover, as part of the contract, the client is assured agents will reliably replicate the script on the phone. Clients are sent updates from the three sets of statistics in the form of bar charts and, from time to time, the client asks for redrafts of the script if progress and results are unsatisfactory. As a result, contractual agreement regarding agents' fidelity to the master script matters to the client because it undergirds the production of statistics demonstrating a campaign's progress. It indicates CallCentral's commitment to fulfilling the client's demands once the script has been approved and the campaign moves into action.

The campaign managers' descriptions of the processes provide a picture of an institutional system and organization characterized by what sociologists call rationalization. Applying the McDonaldization framework developed by Ritzer (2000) for studying rationalization in modern organizations, call center researchers such as Cameron (2000a) and Korczynski (2001) argue that call centers are characterized by four rationalization characteristics, namely: "calculability," "predictability," "efficiency," and "control." So far the processes described suggest all four apply to the call center. The generation of statistics is a process of "calculation" based on predicted goals. The statistical tabulations allow analysis and comparison in the service of these target goals. Furthermore, the early "predictions" made by management are intended to ensure "efficiency" on the part of the agent and in the call center's use of resources. Finally, statistics are also needed to ensure "control" for both the client and management over what is happening on the phone and to monitor progress. On a more general level, clients' motivation in using call center services is based at least in part on the center's ability to offer steps that meet the four rationalization characteristics, thereby guaranteeing measurable results through convergence rate calculations and statistics.

The actual production or entextualization of the script occurs in this context of managerial expectations. I explore this process next and address the ways in which campaign mangers' knowledge of the system affects their participation.

The production of the script

Campaign managers say that the script's production consists of three activities. In the first, the sales meeting, the company's sales person and the client meet to agree on the contract and the broad contours of the script. In the second activity, script drafting, the campaign manager writes the first draft of the script using the texts from the first activity. In the third activity, client

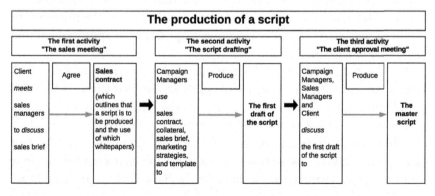

Fig. 3.4   The production of a script. (Source: Woydack and Rampton 2016)

approval meeting, the script is finalized with the client, sales, and the campaign managers. They all meet to discuss the draft and agree on the final version for the master script. This is summarized in Figure 3.4.

Step 1: The sales meeting

During the sales meeting, the client and the call center sales person meet and agree on specific details for the contract and the subsequent proceedings. The client comes to the meeting with a written sales brief that summarizes their wishes and priorities for the campaign. Figure 3.5 lists some of the contractual terms discussed. Each of the different contractual elements, apart from the sales brief itself, has its own price tag that feeds into the overall cost of the campaign (cf. Woydack and Rampton 2016). As a general rule, pricing is based on the notion that the more detailed and specific the information required, the more expensive a campaign will be. The justification for this is

---

1) **Sales brief:** A summary of client's needs and wishes that gives a preliminary view of the type of leads, lead criteria, and collaterals

2) **Leads:** An indicator that the agent has successfully contacted the desired person within the particular company and managed to obtain all the required information

   a) **Type:** The call center distinguishes between three types of leads:
   Engagement leads: Agents do not need to obtain any information apart from contact details and company details (company size, industry, address)
   BANT leads: Agents need to ask several (profiling) questions regarding a potential project plus they need to obtain contact details and company details (company size, industry, address)
   Nurturing leads: Agents need to ask a long list of very specific detailed technical questions regarding a potential project, issues, and needs, plus they need to obtain contact details and company details (company size, industry, address)

   b) **Criteria:** The lead criteria specify:
   • which questions agents need to ask
   • which company size, industry, and job titles are to be targeted.

   > The questions, company size, job titles and industry should be listed on the script

   c) **Quantity and deadlines :** There is a discussion of how many leads need to be generated and by when. The call center will predict how many leads they can generate, the staff they will need to employ, and the associated costs, and it will charge the client accordingly.

3) **Collaterals:** This is the information e.g., a whitepaper, reports, a webinar that the client wants the call center to send to the target audience. It is the "bait," so to speak, to attract the interest of the person called.

4) **Script:** It is agreed that the call center produces a script based on the client's sales brief, collaterals, and details of the sales contract.

5) **Dial rates:** Statistical information based on call outcomes logged by agents after each call. It is useful information for the client to understand how the script (campaign and company) is perceived by the target audience. The numbers of how many dials agents should make per day is decided during the meeting.

Fig. 3.5 Contractual terms discussed and agreed on in sales meeting. (Adapted from Woydack and Rampton 2016)

Table 3.2 Contractual agreements for the BIS campaign

Client name	"Best Internet Security (BIS)"
Targets	4,000 engagement leads in total across the UK, France, Germany [engagement leads=information on company and contact details]
Company size	50–1000 employees
Industry	All
Target audience	All IT professionals and job titles including IT Support
Timeframe	One month but with weekly delivery of engagement leads
Possible collaterals [items the client wants the call center to send to the targets]	One whitepaper/report on SBP—Safe Browsing Policy to be basis of agent's script
Budget of campaign	£25 a lead (cheapest kind of leads) Overall budget £100,000
Dials	200 a day per agent
Script	1 Engagement script—no profiling questions in the pitch (the main section of the script)

Adapted from Woydack and Rampton (2016)

that greater information needs require skilled agents, longer collection times, and more manpower.

In the BIS campaign, several contractual elements were agreed upon (see Table 3.2). The contract includes an agreement about which collateral(s) a client would like to be emailed. Regarding this, the client will have brought a range of these, such as reports or e-books that support a service or sale, and the client and upstairs decide which should be offered (and become the focus of the campaign). In the case of the BIS campaign, the client and upstairs agree on a whitepaper/report on Safe Browsing Policy (SBP). Overall, agreements reached during the sales meeting are summarized in the sales contract signed by the two parties. After the agreement is signed, the campaign managers start drafting the reference script, the next activity, drawing on the client's sales brief, sales contract, and the agreed collateral(s). Most likely, none of the campaign managers will have been present during the sales meeting and hence they will need these texts (sales brief, sales contract, collateral(s)) to draft a script that meets the client's wishes. In the next subsection I explore the script drafting in more detail.

Step 2: The script drafting

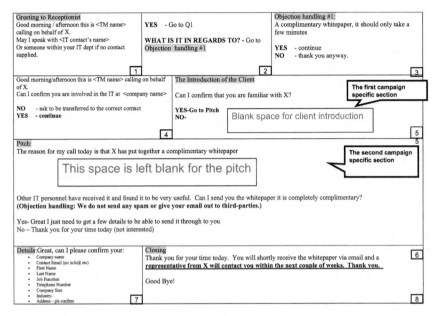

Fig. 3.6   The template for scripts. (Source: Woydack and Rampton 2016)

According to campaign managers, script drafting consists of two parts. The first part is a pre-set template, always produced in English, that campaign managers follow (Figure 3.6). As a second part, the campaign managers then fill in the blank sections.

Both in the template in Figure 3.6 and in the example of a campaign-specific script as shown in Figure 3.7, there are eight fields/textboxes. Seven of the eight text boxes are considered separate sections. These seven represent different stages within the call and have their own headings. The first is entitled **Greeting to the Receptionist** (1), followed by possible **Objection Handling** when speaking to the receptionist (3). Textbox 2 instructs agents that if they do not face any rebuttals, they can skip textbox (3). Agents then **Introduce** themselves to the target contact person (4). and introduce the client on whose behalf they are calling (**The Introduction of the Client**) (5). The **Pitch** (6) represents the centerpiece

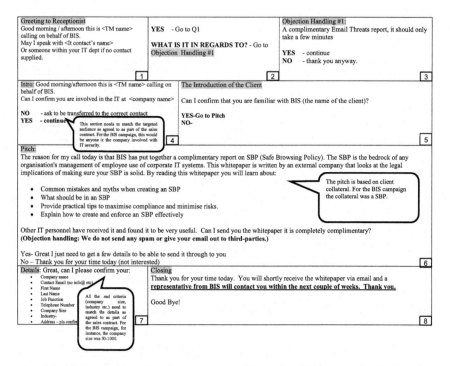

Fig. 3.7 An example of a campaign-specific script (BIS campaign). (Source: Woydack and Rampton 2016)

of the script, followed by the confirmation of **Details** (7) and the **Closing** (8). The blank spaces on the template indicate the only parts to be newly drafted from campaign to campaign, these being the **"pitch"** (6) and **"the introduction of the client"** (5). As part of the drafting process, the campaign managers work their way through the template and fill in the blank spaces. The script in Figure 3.7 provides an example of how campaign managers refer back to specific parts of texts from the sales meeting such as the sales contract, and entextualize and recontextualize them.

Table 3.3 below demonstrates that for every campaign-specific production, there is a fixed process to decide the design of the script and the content of each textbox.

Specifically, when it comes to composition, campaign managers follow a range of strategies advocated in textbooks on business talk that guide them in deciding which parts of the text from the sales meeting should be

Table 3.3 Textboxes on the script and their source

Title of each textbox of the script	Source
The introduction to the receptionist	Template
Objection handling	Template
Introduction to the contact	Template
Introduction of the client	Sales brief, corporate website, info provided by the company.
Pitch	Template, collateral (e.g., whitepaper), sales agreement, sales brief
Details	Template, sales brief, sales agreement contract
Closing	Template

Source: Woydack and Rampton (2016)

embedded in the script to make it successful. This becomes clear when I compare the strategies the campaign managers mentioned in interviews and with business textbooks.

First and foremost, campaign managers identify the main points of a contract and of the collaterals. To identify the main points of the collaterals, the campaign managers try to find out what they are about and highlight the benefits of the product(s) or issues discussed. Laura explains:

Extract 3.9

Then we go through the collaterals that we need to present from the client. And we try to find the core of it, so what's the solution of the product or the problem about, what, reading this White Paper or listening to this webcast, will they learn about, so what's the benefit about it, which is like why they should say "yes" to receiving it. And then, then we just finish off for a minute there the rest of the script. (*Laura, campaign manager*)

Like Laura, Jenny says that the first step is to identify the topic within the resources provided. She believes this to be important because she considers talking directly about the product the client sells to be bad practice. Instead, the pitch should be framed as a service enquiry by focusing on the audience's potential needs and problems, and the benefits of the solution. In addition, it should aim for personal relevance, for instance, by using a personal pronoun like *you*. Jenny's suggestions can be summarized as:

- "The tone" of the script should not be direct
- Questions should be carefully phrased
- Focus on benefits of solutions rather than product
- Create personal relevance and relevance to the company
- Don't mention the product the client actually sells such as software or hardware [SBP is a policy guideline not a product- it is the bait]
- Promote topic over product

Both Jenny's and Laura's strategies are in line with strategies that can be found in general textbooks about business talk. For instance, *Lesikar's Basic Business Communication* (2001) makes similar recommendations:

Like Jenny and Laura, this textbook also suggests making "scripts memorable" with "a good introduction" (gain attention), talking "about benefits" and promoting the relevant "topic" (the persuasion), and making "it [the pitch] relevant to them [the listener] and their company" (you-viewpoint) (Lesikar et al. 2001, 161). In another book, *The Ultimate Book of Phone Scripts* (2010, 15–17), author Mike Brooks, an experienced salesman and consultant, follows the same principles advocated by Laura and Jenny and the textbook by Lesikar and colleagues (Lesikar et al. 2001). Not only does Brooks (2010) dedicate several chapters to "how to have a 'smart opening' on the phone," he also lists "five ways to sound more natural on the phone (2010, 15)." In the extract below, I have again underlined the strategies and wordings reminiscent of Laura's and Jenny's (Brooks 2010, 15–17).

Requests that are likely to be resisted, require a slow deliberate approach. The direct order suggested for routine requests just will not do the job. Persuasion is necessary. By persuasion, we mean reasoning with the reader—presenting facts and logic that support your case. In this approach, which is discussed in detail below, you should generally follow this indirect plan:

- Open with words that (1) set up the strategy and (2) gain attention
- Present the strategy (the persuasion), using persuasive language and you-viewpoint.
- Make the requests clearly and without negatives (1) either at the end of the message or (2) followed by words that recall the persuasive appeal (Lesikar et al. 2001, 161)

1. **Always use the prospect's first name**
   (...)
2. **Be polite**
   (...) Words like "please" and "thank you" go a long way when trying to make a connection with a prospect, and they work especially well when you're trying to get through a gatekeeper. Examine your current scripts now and do all you can to insert the proper courtesies.
3. <u>Be brief</u>
   (...) I review scripts all the time that are essentially a dissertation of a company's brochure. You can turn that around and sound so much better with a brief presentation and checking in with your prospect. Try these scripts.
   "Briefly _____, <u>the reason I'm calling</u> is that we've been working with many companies like yours, and I just wanted to see if we could help you as well. Can I ask you a couple of questions to see if we'd be a fit for you? (...)
4. **Make a connection**
   This is one of the easiest of all and it's a great way to get your prospect talking. All you do is find something that you know is affecting your clients (like new laws in their industry), and ask how it's affecting your new prospects. (...)
5. **Listen more**
   (...)

(Brooks 2010, 15–17) [emphasis added]

> Similar wording to the script (figure) and template (figure) "the reason I'm calling"

Set in the larger institutional context I have described, the script drafting presents several challenges for the campaign managers:

- They were not present at the sales meeting, and had not heard all the details.
- The institutional system prioritizes the client's wishes and interpretation.
- The contractual understanding does not consider the fact that texts travel and that they have to be reinterpreted by the participants in the process; as a result, they take on different significances.
- Texts emerging from the sales meeting (sales contract) as the basis of the master script (sales contract, sales brief, and collaterals) are often described by campaign managers as too impractical to be implemented.

In the remainder of this chapter and the next two chapters, I explore how these challenges are resolved. As Laura's quote below (Extract 3.10) indicates, the campaign managers know well that contractually, the most important thing is to produce a written script that pleases the client.

Extract 3.10

> When we write the script we need to think about the client as well so the client wants to see something in the script that someone on the phone might not necessarily want to hear. (*Laura, campaign manager*)

Let us now turn very briefly indeed to the final activity in the production of the master script, the client approval meeting.

Step 3: The client approval meeting

Although in this meeting there might be some discussion about the draft the client has been sent in advance of the meeting, and although the campaign manager may complain that the texts from the first sales meeting are impractical for use, the client most likely will force through what they believe is the best version of the script, and this will become the master script. The client envisions, then, that the agents will read from the master script word for word. Clients seldom consider the dynamics of communication within which a script must be implemented on the phone. Campaign managers like Laura are fully aware that once the script travels downstairs, it will not be realistic or practical for agents to use the master script verbatim as the management upstairs and client thinks it should be.

Extract 3.11

> You don't need to read it, you can just make it yours, you can just change and see it's… like maybe, if you are the target audience, maybe talking to you in a conversation you don't say something because the conversation just flows in a different way and with me it's different so I expect them to… not to follow it completely word by word. (…) So I expect agents to [change the script]… because one of the most important things for me is to sound colloquial. (*Laura, campaign manager*) (Source: Woydack and Rampton 2016)

Interim conclusion

In summary, the production of the script follows a set process based on the principles outlined in the section about the contractual expectations. When it comes to the production of a campaign-specific script, the main source is the sales contract, which in large part determines the content. In the final instance, the client always decides on the final version of the script even though the campaign managers produce a draft using a range of compositional strategies advocated in business textbooks. More generally, it seems the management upstairs considers scripts very useful as they help to coordinate individuals across multiple local settings and time (Smith 2001, 160).

The importance that the campaign-specific scripts hold for the call center is underlined when we remember that a script and its accompanying briefs are the only documents/texts that agents and team leaders are given during their employment at the call center. As such, the script is an organizational document that establishes a sense of hierarchy, organizational identity, and rules for the temporary agents, and coordinates people's activities across multiple local settings and time (cf. e.g., Cooren 2004). However, despite upstairs commitments to stable script text, campaign managers conceptualize scripts as needing flexible adaptation. They recognize that along their career, scripts may be transformed by the various participants in line with the premises and contexts within which they are addressed. This situational transpositioning is part of campaign managers' agency. Anwar, for instance, critiques the widespread industry view that static scripts should be read out verbatim.

Extract 3.12

> Personally I think scripts are essential to the business but that doesn't mean forcing agents to read word by word which I consider a very bad industry practice. (*Anwar, campaign manager*)

Although it would be easy to just bash upstairs for incompetence, seeing the master script as part of a trajectory helps to reveal the attitudes upstairs, not as out of touch or incompetent, but as positioned. Using the theory of transposition shows that those upstairs view the master script as regulating the downstairs managers and agents because they "co-ordinate individuals across multiple settings and times." This is an upstairs-centric view derived from the primary upstairs task of drafting or framing the master script in line with client's desires. The framework further shows that seeing the scripts as text regulating activities downstairs is only one framing of the script. Although it is undoubtedly important, it is "upstairs-centric" and potentially limited to locality. Viewed in this way, it is clear that (i) upstairs' orientation toward the script is different from that of the employees downstairs as their vantage point is determined by a prioritization of the client's needs, (ii) their orientation, which includes rationalization, is produced within different premises and activities than those of the campaign managers downstairs who operate in line with more pragmatic rationalization, and (iii) upstairs managers are not involved in the script's career stages downstairs, except perhaps to critique performances when targets are not met.

In this chapter, I have taken the production of the script as the initial focus and point of departure in its career, because the point of the meeting was to produce a "durable and authoritative" text (Bauman 1996) and in line with the client's wishes. In the next chapter I address the dynamics of the transformation of a script during implementation as it moves into the call center downstairs.

References

Bauman, Richard. 1996. Transformations of the Word in the Production of Mexican Festival Drama. In *Natural Histories of Discourse*, ed. Michael Silverstein and Greg Urban, 301–329. Chicago/London: Chicago University Press.

Brooks, Mike. 2010. *The Ultimate Book of Phone Scripts*. Georgia: Thomson.

Cameron, Deborah. 2000a. *Good to Talk?* London: Sage.

———. 2000b. Styling the Worker: Gender and the Commodification of Language in the Globalized Service Economy. *Journal of SocioLinguistics* 4 (3): 323–347.

Cooren, Francois. 2004. Textual Agency: How Texts Do Things in Organizational Settings. *Organization* 11 (3): 373–393.

Farrell, Lesley. 2009. Texting the Future: Work Literacies, New Economy and Economies. In *The Future of Literacy Studies*, ed. Mike Baynham and Mastin Prinsloo, 181–199. Basingstoke: Palgrave Macmillan.

Johnstone, Barbara. 2003. The Linguistic Individual in an American Public Opinion Survey. In *Sociolinguistics – The Essential Readings*, ed. C.B. Paulston and R. Tucker, 272–286. Oxford: Blackwell.

Korczynski, Marek. 2001. The Contradictions of Service Work: The Call Centre as a Consumer Oriented Bureaucracy. In *Customer Service – Control, Colonisation and Contradiction*, ed. A. Sturdy, I. Grugilis, and H. Wilmott, 79–101. London: Macmillan.

Lesikar, Raymond Vincent, John D. Pettit, and Marie Elizabeth Flatley. 2001. *Lesikar's Basic Business Communication*. 5th ed., International ed. Boston: Irwin/McGraw-Hill.

Ritzer, George. 2000. *The McDonaldization of Society*. New Century ed. Thousand Oaks: Pine Forge Press.

Smith, Dorothy E. 2001. Texts and the Ontology of Organizations and Institutions. *Studies in Cultures, Organizations and Societies* 7 (2): 159–198.

Woydack, Johanna. 2016. Superdiversity and a London Multilingual Call Centre. In *Engaging Superdiversity: Recombining Spaces, Times and Language Practices*, 7, ed. Karel Arnaut, Martha Sif Karrebaek, Massimiliano Spotti, and Jan Blommaert, 220–251. Bristol: Multilingual Matters.

Woydack, Johanna, and Ben Rampton. 2016. Text Trajectories in a Multilingual Call Centre: The Linguistic Ethnography of a Calling Script. *Language in Society* 45 (05): 709–732.

4

The Second Stage in the Script's Career: Adaptation of the Master Script

Introduction

The last chapter focused on the production of the master script. There we saw how the script, complemented by a range of electronic text-mediated technologies, is crucial in creating a local order of accountability, compatible with the sales contract. This chapter explores how upstairs now uses the text of the master script to regulate and co-ordinate "courses of actions" in the call center itself (cf. Smith 1996, 177). Hitherto, we have seen that the production of the master script is marked by different orientations and potential disagreement between the three main parties encountered so far: the client (e.g., Field note entry 1.1), the management upstairs, and the campaign managers. The client and upstairs expect the master script to be read word for word by its users downstairs and not to be changed. Conversely, the campaign managers predict the master script will become subject to oral and textual transformations as it is taken up by different agents across various settings and activities.

Set against this backdrop, I describe the next stage of the script's career, its adaptation in terms of (i) activities underpinning the second stage, (ii) participants' orientation towards the master script, and (iii) changes to the master script itself.

© The Author(s) 2019
J. Woydack, *Linguistic Ethnography of a Multilingual Call Center:*
London Calling, Communicating in Professions and Organizations,
https://doi.org/10.1007/978-3-319-93323-8_4

In terms of the script's career and the anonymized BIS model campaign, two sets of activities (two briefings) occur during which the BIS master script is taken up by groups of new participants (campaign managers, team leaders, and agents) who, with the exception of the campaign manager, have not been involved in the master script's production. The ground covered is diagrammed in Figure 4.1. Before I begin, I briefly introduce the informants and describe the monitoring that is pervasive at this level.

The information in this chapter comes from several sources. In addition to my field notes and training documents, I draw on interviews I conducted with the campaign managers and team leaders. The interviews with the agents form the focus of the next chapter. The team leaders I interviewed were:

- *Stuart,* the team leader for Jenny's campaigns. He is the most senior and experienced of the current team leaders and is now in charge of the high-end nurturing campaigns.
- *Ada,* the team leader for Laura's campaigns.
- *Siiri,* a substitute team leader brought in to help out during peak times like Christmas. She reports to Laura.
- *Barbara,* a substitute team leader who helps out during peak times; she is otherwise doing quality control. She reports to Jenny.
- *Claudia,* a former team leader.
- *Piia,* a former team leader.

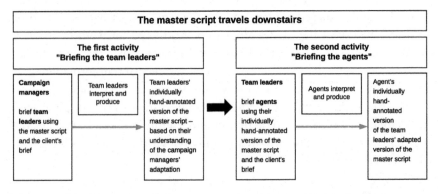

Fig. 4.1   The adaptation of the master script. (Source: Woydack and Rampton 2016)

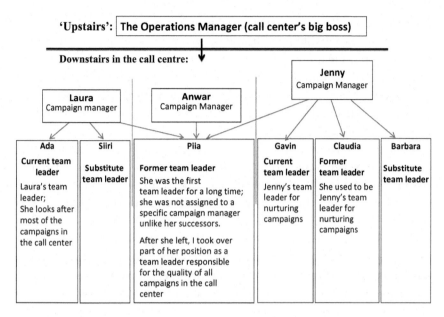

'Upstairs': | The Operations Manager (call center's big boss)

Downstairs in the call centre:

Jenny
Campaign Manager

Laura
Campaign manager

Anwar
Campaign Manager

Ada	Siiri	Piia	Gavin	Claudia	Barbara
Current team leader Laura's team leader; She looks after most of the campaigns in the call center	**Substitute team leader**	**Former team leader** She was the first team leader for a long time; she was not assigned to a specific campaign manager unlike her successors. After she left, I took over part of her position as a team leader responsible for the quality of all campaigns in the call center	**Current team leader** Jenny's team leader for nurturing campaigns	**Former team leader** She used to be Jenny's team leader for nurturing campaigns	**Substitute team leader**

Fig. 4.2   The hierarchy in the call center. (Adapted from Woydack and Rampton 2016)

The relations between the campaign managers and the team leaders can be visualized using Figure 4.2.

Before exploring the process of text adaptation in more detail, I address monitoring. I begin with the operations manager's expectations concerning monitoring, which he once told me in a one-to-one meeting. Then I move on to the team leaders' perception of this matter.

Living with monitoring from management upstairs

According to the operations manager, the management upstairs expects the campaign managers and team leaders to ensure (i) that agents reproduce the master script during their calls word for word and interpret it as the client intended and that (ii) the regulation and co-ordination of agents' activities downstairs is in line with a procedure fixed by upstairs managers. The procedure is supposed to begin with the campaign managers "briefing" the respective team leaders on the campaign. During the briefing, two documents should be covered, the master script, which is read aloud to team leaders, and the client's brief outlining targets and any useful background information about the campaign. Once the team leaders have been briefed, they are expected to provide the same briefing to agents. Team leaders must also ensure that all agents have their own copy of the printed master script. This is important so that agents can read from it verbatim and the corresponding statistics including dial reports can be generated. The generated dial reports can be compared to the predictions made for the specific master script for generating statistics. If we return to the example of the anonymized BIS campaign, it is predicted that every agent makes 15 leads and 200 dials a day, with a lead call lasting at least three minutes. If the statistics reveal that agents do not make either of these target numbers, the call monitor downstairs will be asked to listen to their calls and drill deeper to "fix the problem." If the issue persists, the agent should be laid off. Otherwise, there is a risk that the agent could increase the overall cost of the campaign by requiring more time than calculated and covered by the campaign's budget. For this reason, team leaders need to report back every day to their campaign managers about each agent's performance. Based on the team leaders' accounts and the statistics, the campaign managers then compile their own reports for the daily six o'clock evening meeting upstairs with their managers.

Field note entry 4.1 provides an illustration of the notion of monitoring held by upstairs operations managers. Since the operations manager expects team leaders and agents to read directly from the script, he does not mention a possible adaptation. Instead, his account stresses the need for team leaders to monitor agents so targets are met and the statistics sold to the client and calculated on the basis of the approved master script are reliable indicators of campaign progress. From an upstairs point of view, it is important that agents meet their targets for the client. What do the team leaders think of this monitoring?

Team leaders do not criticize monitoring per se, but rather the fact that it is impersonal, inflexible, and that there is no regard for particular pressures at certain times. They also believe that there is insensitivity to the

Field Note Entry 4.1 The operations manager's view of monitoring

After lunch I received a message telling me to come to the panic room for a meeting. Jenny and the operations manager were there looking at statistics. The operations manager was complaining to Jenny that agents on the BIS campaign (at that moment the biggest campaign in the call center) had neither made enough calls nor leads. He also asked me why the lead and dial results were so low given that reading the script on the phone lasts only two and a half minutes. With such a short script, he claimed agents could make many more calls than they did. He ordered me to make sure that my fellow team leaders enforced the dial rates.

Given that it was the team leaders' job to report back to the management every afternoon, he got annoyed that no one upstairs had been alerted to the problems on the BIS campaign. He seemed to blame me (and my fellow team leaders) for this lack of communication and the subsequent poor results. He looked me deep in the eye and told me with a serious voice that it was essential that the team leaders and I ... report back to our campaign managers in the future. I apologized and promised to do so (although of course everything had been reported back to the campaign managers and Jenny knew that). Jenny did not say anything, but it was clear to me that her strategy was, as she had done before, to blame the poor results on "unsackable" (difficult to replace) team leaders to ensure that none of the agents were being fired by the operations manager. The real reason for the lack of results was the poor data [the phone numbers in the lists that agents use for calling], which included many invalid numbers as well as private numbers, making it impossible for agents to have a high dial or lead rate, and she did not share this with the operations manager as she said he would not understand it anyway. He had never worked on the phone himself. In addition, the call center had spent a lot of money on purchasing new data which now turned out to be not that good.

Once the operations manager had gone back upstairs, Jenny apologized to me about what had happened in the panic room. She knew, of course, that it was neither my fault nor the fault of any of the other team leaders. She needed more time to fix the campaign and to prevent the operations manager from "sending anyone home."

unavoidable variability in individual performance in the face of the same set of high targets every day. Specifically, there are four points of criticism.

First, combined targets of dial rates and lead targets are regarded as being unrealistic, inflexible, incompatible, and unachievable. As Barbara notes:

Extract 4.1

Targets are always kept at a level which are pretty much impossible to hit (…) yes, it's stressful (…) I would find it more beneficial if such targets could be kind of ordered on and off, modified, sometimes brought a bit down, because obviously you know… the management knows what can be hit [management uses unrealistic targets as a managerial motivational tool—Barbara talks about this later in the interview] and what cannot be, and sometimes they can be unrealistic and that can frustrate you as well because you know that there's no point even trying harder because I'm not going to hit that. I think sometimes they should be a bit more realistic (…). It's fine to have them high but I think they should be high to a point where they can still be achievable and realistic (…) everybody's different and one person might be able to dial 250 dials a day and one person just cannot do more than 150. Sometimes people do 120 and they get more, many more leads than people who are doing 200/250 dials. So I think we can't like put everyone in one box but we should have like an average around which we should have like room for people who are falling within that range, you know, and not too far below basically. (*Barbara, substitute team leader*)

Second, the technology behind the monitoring system is perceived as inadequate. For instance, Ada suggests that it only tells half the story of what happens on the phone.

Extract 4.2

I'm not listening to their calls. If I see someone with like 120 dials when it's like three o'clock or four o'clock and things like that, sometimes I feel bad. I don't want to actually come out and say, "Yeah, you need to pick up your dials," and things like that, because at the end of the day, I don't know why you have the number of dials you have; I don't know the people you have been speaking with. I check that if you have lengthy conversations, what am I supposed to say? I can see it on the system [from the statistics] that you've had lengthy conversations with people; I'm not going to tell you, "Yeah, if the person's talking too much cut them off." (*Ada, senior team leader*)

Third, the dial rate targets on their own are described as not feasible. Both Siiri and Ada agree that this is the case for the dial rates for engagement campaigns in particular, like BIS.

Extract 4.3

There's no way people can actually get 200 dials. (*Ada, senior team leader*)

Siiri explicitly criticizes the exclusively quantitative assessment of performance which takes no account of quality.

Extract 4.4

I've actually counted it once because one of my friends was like I can't reach 200 dials no matter what I do, and I've reached it maybe once but maybe I've talked to two people like besides the gatekeeper. (…) It's like do you want more quantity or do you want quality? So (…) it depends exactly what you want because if you want quality leads, then you're not going to get 200 dials per day, that's I think just a fact (…). So if they want always 200 dials (…) So I think it was per person, per dials, like two and a half minutes, two minutes, [per dial and person you cannot talk longer than two and a half minutes] to get to that target (…) Some people can do it, but they're not, you know, they're not talking to anyone, yeah. (*Siiri, substitute team leader*)

Importantly, Siiri contradicts the operation managers' calculations cited earlier. We saw that he had estimated that reading the BIS script word for word should last three minutes and that agents should be able to make 200 dials a day. Siiri, nonetheless, says that she counted it once and for an agent to meet their target of 200 dials a day, the average call, including a lead call, cannot be longer than two and a half minutes.

With targets perceived as unrealistic, the question emerges, how do team leaders cope with monitoring? Field note entry 4.2 describes what can happen when the operations manager visits.

Field Note Entry 4.2 Visits by the operations manager: pressure on meeting increased targets and coping with them

[The operations manager came downstairs from time to time. He often also came to talk to me as he was my direct line manager since I was responsible for the quality of the campaigns. Prior to my first one-to-one meeting with him, Jenny had warned me that whenever I dealt with him, I needed to remember that he had no idea what was going on in the call center or what working on the phone involved. He spends all his day looking at numbers and estimating things. At the same time, it is his job to try to lower costs and bring up the call center's revenue.] These are the notes I took of one of my meetings with him:

That day the operations manager came downstairs to have a chat with me in one of the meeting rooms about targets at the end of the quarter. I was very proud of what we as a group of team leaders had achieved that quarter, as we were in all campaigns on or above target, but without having put too much pressure on agents. However, looking over the results for that day, he pointed at the performance of one of the star agents called Sonia. For that day, she had already hit her target of 15 leads a day (she had made 17 leads at that point). He then asked me the rhetorical question of how I would double her performance today, if I were the operations manager. To my horror, he then ordered me to go up to her (it was 4 p.m.) and tell her that she should try to hit 30 leads in the next hour; otherwise she would not get her incentive.

After the meeting, I talked to Ada about what had happened. She was rather upset and angry. We agreed that I would talk about it to Jenny, as the most powerful person downstairs.

Jenny told me to ignore him and just do my thing. She would talk to him to ensure that he would never bother me again. She is very happy with me and the job I do, that is all that matters. She told me that everybody just ignores him as he is incompetent and I should do the same. (Adapted from Woydack and Rampton 2016)

Since the intervention of the operations manager is perceived as unfair and driven by unrealistic expectations, his requests are met with anger and resistance, and are typically ignored.

Another mechanism for coping is what is known downstairs as the "voicemail strategy," which essentially is a short cut for agents and team leaders to increase their dial rates without calling properly. Its benefit is that it is almost impossible to spot from the statistics. The idea is to primarily log, track, and call back numbers that probably no one will answer (voicemails). Without any unpredictable human interaction, an agent can make many valid calls in a minute but long enough that the calls do not appear to be "dummy calls" (see Chapter 2). For example, Claudia explains:

Extract 4.5

> For instance, I remember on the DDC campaign […] I had the operations manager on my case because Jenny was on holiday (…) I took readings [of the time I spend on the phone for each call] (…) the one ring, two ring, three ring (…) [and no one picks up the phone], boom, next. (…) I used to track voicemail and put VM, VM, VM, VM [so she will have a list of calls she logged as voicemails—where no one picked up the phone]. So that at some point of the day I used to go back just on voicemail [and call all the numbers again which were voicemail as most likely they were still on voice-mail. This allows her to make 10 calls in one minute as there will be no long human interaction], that could help me in increasing my reachability and my target [she can then spend the time she gained from the VM strat-egy on numbers where she knows she might be able to talk to someone in person and make a lead and meet her lead targets too] in terms of numbers. (*Claudia, former team leader*)

Despite these attempts to cope, team leaders still report that the pressures of monitoring impact the adaptation of the master script. As Field note entry 4.3 shows, this is frequently the case at the end of the quarter.

Field note entry 4.3 shows that the pressure of unrealistic monitoring, including higher targets, can mean the master script gets pared down (see also Woydack and Rampton 2016). Later, I will show examples of this in role plays. These role plays stem from interviews during which I asked informants to simulate role plays that would occur in these meetings and during training.

Sometimes the gaps between upstairs' and downstairs' understandings of monitoring and the master script become conspicuous (see Field note entry 4.4).

The gap is systematically managed by the campaign managers, for they know that upstairs will not find out about the shortcuts taken with the script for three reasons. First, they cannot listen to calls downstairs as

Field Note Entry 4.3 The impact of monitoring on the master script at the end of the quarter

So far it had not been a very stressful day and the atmosphere in the call center was very relaxed. The team leaders thought everyone was on track when it came to targets.

During lunch, the entire call center management goes upstairs for a meeting that lasts two hours. Once they come back downstairs, Jenny calls all the substitute team leaders, team leaders who help out, to the panic room.

Following the panic room meeting, the substitute team leaders walked around the call center with a piece of paper, reprimanding specific agents, all on UK engagement campaigns, such as the BIS campaign, that they needed to make more dials as upstairs had increased the dial rates again (to 250 dials instead of 200). Jenny also shouted some names across the call center identifying individuals who, according to the dial sheet, were not doing well, while swearing about sales upstairs. There was some confusion downstairs among the team leaders about what the actual new targets were with everyone saying something else. Agents also panicked. They complained that the targets were impossible and if the dial rates are so high, they would have to leave out a lot of sentences from the master script and only stick to the skeleton.

At one point, Ada came to the bubble room to talk to me about how we were going to handle the even more unrealistic targets and the fact that agents have started leaving out huge chunks from the script, with calls being too short now. We agree on what needs to be mentioned and what can be left out. As Ada says, no one can expect agents to talk for long on the phone with such high targets. We then get all the agents involved to the panic room and de-brief them. (Adapted from Woydack and Rampton 2016)

monitoring only happens downstairs. Second, the dial sheet available to them does not show the time agents spend on the phone. Third, a client's call back to a lead is highly unlikely to reveal that agents have not read the script word by word.

Taking an analytical step back, we can say that the monitoring system implemented downstairs is based on a scientific notion of reproducibility and accounting (cf. Smith 1996, 181). In fact, it is similar to what Smith (Smith 1996, 181) described for large-scale corporations:

[Within the reality of large-scale corporation management] [t]he replication of local events as identical (though identity is always more or less a

Field Note Entry 4.4 The operations manager's unannounced visits to the call center

From time to time, the operations manager from upstairs (the call center's big boss) would come unannounced downstairs. He would then take a seat among the agents and work from there for a few hours on his laptop. The operations manager called this a "hands on approach."

He always took advantage of the fact none of the agents knew who he was. Despite his seniority, he is only a little bit older than the average call center agent and also dressed casually like everyone else. It is also not uncommon for IT technicians to come to the call center and fix computers without interacting or introducing themselves to agents. So it would not be really strange for agents to see a random guy sitting among them, who would not talk to them, but only type on his laptop.

When the operations manager took a seat downstairs, he remained a nameless figure, talking to none of the agents and like the Holy Spirit, he just came and vanished again. However, the result of these sit-ins was that he was usually very very upset about what he saw happening "uncensored" downstairs.

If Jenny knew he was coming or that he was already there, she was suddenly very strict. The team leaders also tried to give secret warnings to agents that they had to be careful what they did around him. Jenny used to say that we needed to behave according to his rules and ideas when he was around. But once he had gone we could go back to normal, breathe, and have fun again. This is what literally happened today, once he had finally gone back upstairs. It was so nice that one could move and talk again freely around the call center.

fiction) makes possible, for example, systems of measurement, the accumulation of statistical data, the formulation of rules and instructions applicable from one setting and time to others, and other textual practices of science, management and the market. (…) Control of production process at the level of shop floor is tied into accounting systems and other computerized technologies of management that render the company operable within the field of capitalist social relations. (…) Accounting is more than a source of information traveling between work organization at the level of the shop floor to the decision-making level of corporate executives and financial managers. It is an actual organizer of the relations articulating people's work, particularly the processes of production and sales but also of management (…). Accounting and related textual technologies of management coordinate local work processes at the shop floor level (…). (Smith 1996, 181–182)

Upstairs' notion of accountability is built on their belief in identical replication of a master script in every call. The problem for downstairs is that not only are the estimated targets unfeasible, but it is unrealistic for team leaders and agents to read the master script verbatim on the phone on every call. So campaign managers have to mediate between expectations from upstairs and team leaders and agents' need for flexibility. Despite their mediation, monitoring affects the way the script is handled. Let us turn now to this in more detail. How are the team leaders and agents briefed on the master script?

The adpation of the master script in its transition downstairs

Briefing consists of two activities: "briefing the team leaders" and "briefing the agents." In both, adaptation of the master script is the central concern. The master script acquires a range of new forms and meanings.

Step 4: Briefing the team leaders

The team leaders' briefing usually takes place in the panic room. Little time is devoted to this task as campaign managers expect team leaders to be well versed in the use of master scripts. Many team leaders still "work the lines" (make calls) themselves. At the start of the meeting, team leaders receive the typed blank (unannotated) master script, freshly printed, as well as the clients' brief. The campaign managers cover the brief first. The brief conveys the targets and the background information about the client. Team leaders take notes on a notepad they are required to bring to every briefing. A reading of the master script by the campaign manager follows. During the reading, team leaders listen for emphases and significant ideas. They may underline sentences or words that they or the campaign managers deem important and may annotate the document by scribbling down key words mentioned by the campaign manager. These annotations may include personal notes of things a team leader considers important for the clearest communication on the phone. At the meeting's end, every team leader has a typed copy of the master script with their own hand-written annotations. This is now considered his/her "own" script.

Below, the anonymized BIS campaign illustrates such a meeting. Campaign managers would likely point out the following:

The brief

- The customer is one of the call center's best clients
- Brief summary/description of BIS
- All industries can be targeted, company size 50-1000
- Target all job titles in the IT Department
- Goal: 2000 UK leads, 1000 leads in France and Germany
- A definition of SBP (Safe Browsing Policy)

The master script

- BIS is a leading provider of internet security
- 1 whitepaper/report on Safe Browsing Policy (SBP)—how companies manage their digital footprint—written by an independent company
- Benefits (bullet points) in the pitch

How would this material be covered in the briefing? Two of the campaign managers commented on their general approach to briefings. Laura says:

Extract 4.6

When I train them and usually when I read the script to them, I make it… I show them straight away that I'm cutting points and tell them I don't expect you to follow every single thing. (*Laura, campaign manager*)

Jenny talks about the fact that many agents might not understand the script's technical language and concepts, and the need to explain them.

Extract 4.7

> It's very important that everyone gets the idea [of the master script], and people don't always understand what they're talking about, especially the new people that come in. So I remember myself, when I first started here I started to read a script about SSL sockets. I had no idea what I was talking about. (*Jenny, campaign manager*)

Beyond this, campaign managers address two strategies in more detail: personalizing the text and emphasizing the interlocutor. As the script moves closer to actual implementation in calls, campaign managers direct team leaders to stick to the basic elements of the script but to personalize them. This is about team leaders' individual preferences and needs. It acknowledges the opportunity for improved success if agents handle the eight sections of the script in ways that suit their personal style and vocabulary. The second strategy, emphasizing the interlocutor, means addressing the person on the phone in a respectful and "consultative" manner. In this approach, the caller learns to focus their conversation on the other person, integrate them, and improvise around the script. Ideally, the other person does not even realize that agents have a script.

This "consultative" approach is applicable only to high-end BANT and nurturing campaigns for which there are many associated questions and long scripts. This approach does not usually apply to engagement campaigns such as the BIS campaign, although to some extent good listening skills are part of a repertoire of communication skills that promote success in calling. I turn now in more detail to the two approaches, personalizing the script and being consultative with one's interlocutor.

Personalization of the master script (making It your own)

Once team leaders have understood the core points of the script, Laura stresses the need for the user to personalize it ("make it your own"). She does not want the team leaders or agents to read the script word for word and sound robotic. Instead, she would like them to fit parts of the script into a conversation.

Extract 4.8

Because if you sound like you are reading, you're a robot, I would say no. So I want them to get used to it, touch on the core points, make it like they... after they memorize, after they know what they're talking about, you don't need to read it, you can just make it yours, you can just change and see it's... like maybe, if you are the target audience, maybe talking to you in a conversation you don't say something because the conversation just flows in a different way and with me it's different so I expect them to... not to follow it completely word by word. (*Laura, campaign manager*)

For her, the script is a basic structure which allows team leaders and agents to make amendments within set boundaries:

Extract 4.9

JW: Are you in favor of using scripts?
L: Yeah, yeah, yeah, completely, because every time it's different (...) we need everyone to have the same structure and then of course you can amend it slightly [within the structure] but you need a structure for that. (*Laura, campaign manager*)

Anwar shares Laura's view of scripts, which he prefers to call "call guides."

Extract 4.10

Personally I think scripts are essential to the business, but that doesn't mean forcing agents to read word by word, which I consider a very bad industry practice. Each individual has their own way of delivering a message and the whole idea of a script is to set guidelines around what needs to be said and asked. That's why I like calling them "Call Guides" instead. (...) We need to make sure all relevant questions are asked in a professional manner and for that reason, a flow is devised in the script to help them stay on track. (*Anwar, campaign manager*) (Source: Woydack and Rampton 2016)

Consultative approach (going beyond the master script)

Jenny described the "consultative approach" in the following way.

Extract 4.11

> When you're pitching to someone, you don't want to waste their time, so it's very, very important that you make the pitch memorable; you have to engage with them on the script, otherwise there's no recall after it; so you need to make sure that you're thinking about positioning the script in a way that you grasp them [the listener] quickly but you don't rattle on to them too much. Then you get them listening and then you could start pitching to them, but you need to listen and pause to hear their [feedback/reaction]... If they're getting bored you need to speed up. If they're asking questions, slow down and answer the questions.

Only top agents, those "good" at personalization and fluent in the language of the market, are trained in this approach. These agents are assigned to campaigns with longer and more complicated scripts. Such agents may also be appointed team leaders. As experienced callers, team leaders also stress that good listening is key to delivering a client's message successfully and is thus a central part of the consultative approach.

These trends in call implementation make monitoring more challenging. Personalization and consultation strategies are valued, yet so are key elements of the script. In the script's structure are headings that show callers should (1) introduce themselves to the receptionist, (2) handle potential objections, (3) introduce themselves to the contact, (4) introduce the client, (5) cover core points of the pitch and profiling questions (6), (7) confirm details, and (8) close the call. These eight sections should always be reflected in a call that runs its full duration (Figure 4.3).

In Chapter 3, we saw that the production of specific scripts focused on two sections. These were the "pitch" and the "introduction of the client," the two campaign sections of the script specifically approved by the client. The information in these two sections is important and will need to

Greeting to Receptionist Good morning / afternoon this is <TM name> calling on behalf of BIS. May I speak with <IT contact's name> Or someone within your IT dept if no contact supplied.	YES - Go to Q1 WHAT IS IT IN REGARDS TO? - Go to Objection Handling #1	Objection Handling #1: A complimentary Email Threats report, it should only take a few minutes YES - continue NO - thank you anyway.
1	**2**	**3**
Intro: Good morning/afternoon this is <TM name> calling on behalf of BIS. Can I confirm you are involved in the IT at <company name> NO - ask to be transferred to the correct contact YES - **continue**	The Introduction of the Client Can I confirm that you are familiar with BIS? YES-Go to Pitch NO-	
4	**5**	

Pitch: The reason for my call today is that BIS has put together a complimentary report on SBP (Safe Browsing Policy). The SBP is the bedrock of any organisation's management of employee use of corporate IT systems. This whitepaper is written by an external company that looks at the legal implications of making sure your SBP is solid. By reading this whitepaper you will learn about: • Common mistakes and myths when creating a SBP • What should be in a SBP • Provide practical tips to maximise compliance and minimise risks. • Explain how to create and enforce a SBP effectively Other IT personnel have received it and found it to be very useful. Can I send you the whitepaper it is completely complimentary? **(Objection handling: We do not send any spam or give your email out to third-parties.)** Yes- Great I just need to get a few details to be able to send it through to you No – Thank you your time today (not interested)
6

Details:Great, can I please confirm your: • Company name • Contact Email (no info@ etc) • First Name • Last Name • Job Function • Telephone Number • Company Size • Industry- • Address – pls confirm	Closing Thank you for your time today. You will shortly receive the whitepaper via email and a **representative from BIS will contact you within the next couple of weeks. Thank you.** Good Bye!
7	**8**

Fig. 4.3 The script as a skeleton or scaffolding

be mentioned during every call. Occasionally a call monitor downstairs or a team leader will listen in on calls to check that agents mention the key points in these two sections and if they follow the structure of the master script (the eight sections).

Former call monitor Piia provides some examples of her practices:

Extract 4.12

Do they actually mention the things what [that] the contact is supposed to know, like what is [the pitch—key section of the script (textbox 6)] really about? So [the pitch] is not just an email, it's the email (…) about something. And then if there was profiling questions, do they really ask the questions [part of the pitch (textbox 6)] and do they ask that they will receive a call back [closing statement (textbox 8)]. (*Piia, former team leader and call monitor*)

Imagining the master script as a skeleton makes the claim possible that agents' calls can be monitored even if they are speaking another language. Piia explains:

Extract 4.13

> I don't know any Arabic, but when I listened to calls in Arabic, I could tell whether agents followed the script because of their intonation. (*Piia, former team leader*). (Source: Woydack 2016)

As I discussed earlier in Chapter 3 (Field note 3.2), team leaders sometimes find it difficult to tell how closely agents are following the content of the master script or what the key points of the pitch are that need to be mentioned. They may sometimes have to guess what is important. However, when clients do the call backs and find that the people called were not told all the information they were supposed to hear, team leaders and agents are taken to task if their version of the master script diverged too far from the skeleton. However, the campaign managers, not the team leaders or agents, would talk to clients to justify and explain any mishaps related to the script without revealing the skeleton strategy. So team leaders, both as monitors and as guides to successful calling, must strike a balance between rote script following and the personalizing and consultative strategies they also advocate.

Downstairs, the master script is not thought of as a fixed product sold to the client. That is, attention has shifted from the precise text to the notion of a general structure or a guideline. Campaign managers encourage team leaders and agents to adapt the words in the master script to make them fit their own way of talking. Expressions like Laura's "make it your own" highlight the difference between downstairs' and upstairs' orientation toward the master script. Team leaders treat their hand-annotated script as their own possession and store it in their pigeon hole to ensure that it does not get thrown away. The regard they show for their own copy illustrates their orientation toward it. Although each agent is given a freshly printed, typed, blank (unannotated) version of the master script for the purpose of the briefing (on which they take notes), the team leader's individually-revised script serves as the basis for training agents. Team leaders can convey the campaign message more convincingly to agents if they use a document they have transformed into a text that they consider both meaningful and likely to be successful in conversations.

However, it must be remembered that the campaign managers and team leaders are walking a delicate line here. While they recognize the importance of modifying a script to suit the conversational style of interlocutors, they must also preserve a facade of sticking to the upstairs management's conception of rote delivery of the script. Below is an example of an incident that occurred while I was working at CallCentral (see Field note entry 4.5). A new team leader, Eva, mistakenly informed a higher level manager of the need for transpositions downstairs. This created somewhat of a stir and required extensive reassurances on the part of more experienced leaders to reestablish the status quo with upper level management. The dual frameworks in which campaign managers and team leaders work creates a stressful and challenging environment for them but one they see as essential to campaign success for the company.

Field Note Entry 4.5 The new campaign manager's faux pas in front of upstairs

Eva, the new campaign manager, was asked to join Jenny, the operations manager from upstairs, and me in the panic room for a meeting. The reason for this panic room meeting was that her campaigns were going very badly and upstairs was getting nervous. During the meeting, Eva said that she felt it was going badly due to the script and that script had to be changed by the agents. At that moment, the operations manager lost it and got very upset. He said that this cannot happen as the script comes from the client. After all, he pointed out the script never gets changed and is read out on all the other campaigns which are successful.

Eva looked very confused and tried to counter the operations manager's words. However, he would not let her. Once the operations manager had left, Jenny went crazy and started shouting at Eva that no one ever changes the script downstairs and asked how she can say something like that in front of the operations manager. After the meeting, Eva came up to me and asked me why Jenny had told her the previous day that agents need to change the script (also in front of me), but she had denied it in front of the operations manager. My reply was that I had observed that one can never say these things in front of upstairs unless one wants to risk anger from them.

Step 5: Briefing the agents and opening the script to transpositions

How is an agent briefing staged, and what strategies do team leaders propose to agents? At the beginning of a briefing, a copy of the master script is given to each agent together with a copy of the client's brief. The master script is always blank and typed, meaning it is not annotated. It is strictly a copy of the script the client approved. Two steps follow: agents are introduced to the client and their campaign (through the client's brief), and then to the master script. This process parallels the team leaders' briefing described earlier.

Extract 4.14

> When I train people I basically, after doing the briefing and so, going through the overview of the client and everything, I go through the entire script. I tell them that if you feel that you have a certain way of saying things and it's not helping, try and change that. If you feel you want to summarize some key points do that. If you feel you want to write down a script in your own words, write it down but have this information in that, you know, the sequence might alter. (*Barbara, substitute team leader*)

Extract 4.15

> When I train people, I try to make it as simple as I can. I still read what's in front of me [the master script] but, after reading like a line, I try to translate it like in a simpler way more like, so if they don't get what's on the script, "Okay, this is what they're saying." I'll put it in layman's terms (...) to help them. (...) I always make sure I tell them [the agents], as long as you don't leave out any vital information (...), you can summarize it [the master script] in a way that they understand it. You understand it clearly, and that's it. (...). One thing I always make sure I talk about when I'm reading the script, I never ever leave out the benefits. Even if you're summarizing anything, always still mention the benefits (...). (*Ada, senior team leader*)

The entire master script is read out to agents, but the team leaders say that they highlight key points to mention on the phone. These are i) the reasons for the call, ii) who they are targeting, and iii) the benefits (of the material to be sent out). How do team leaders cover this material?

The first step is to make a few general comments about the master script itself, including highlighting its eight basic elements. All the team leaders told me they would draw on an analogy to illustrate the script's function to agents. Here are four examples:

(i) Stuart: The master script has parameters which are not set in stone:

Extract 4.16

> The script's constructed in a way that has all the information but also the parameters on the script are not set in stone, you're allowed to change and adapt to your way of talking and your way of getting the information across. I think that's the perfect script. (*Stuart, senior team leader*)

(ii) Siiri: The master script is like a good bible with good and flexible rules:

Extract 4.17

> They [scripts] are good… they're like a good bible, you know, you can… they have good rules and they have a set, a set, you know, target, use this, you know, just outline the most important things and make it your own (…) meaning making it sound like you. (*Siiri, substitute team leader*). (Source: Woydack 2016)

(iii) Ada: The master script as a guideline:

Extract 4.18

Using a script, to be honest with you, I believe it's just like a guideline. At the end of the day, if you give someone a script, I believe the person should use that script, but use it in their own... as in change the words (...) The script thing, as in general is okay because it actually helps people as in, it directs people. (*Ada, senior team leader*) (Source: Woydack 2016)

(iv) Barbara: The master script as a standard with some leeway around it:

Extract 4.19

Because everybody is different and everybody has their own style, so if you make everybody do the same script, it becomes very robotic and nobody wants to hear that on the phone. I think the most successful agents are those who just make it their own; they kind of just get into that role and they just do it naturally, the script is not there, it just comes naturally to them. (...) But yes, that standard should be there; however there should be some leeway around it. (*Barbara, substitute team leader*). (Source: Woydack 2016)

Next, the team leaders train agents who use the skeleton to (i) personalize their calls and (ii) be consultative.

However, before this, team leaders stress that the typed text and format of the master script itself cannot be modified or re-printed. Any adaptation that the team leaders talk about will have to be oral or hand-written as Field note entry 4.6 indicates.

Plainly, all scripts and questions agents present to the IT personal they contact have price tags. That is, the client pays for a specific script, the price of which is calculated on the number of questions to be asked and the depth and detail of those questions. One might assume that added questions would be reflected in adjusted costs to the client, but this is not the case with a hand-written annotation or question, since handwriting indexes something unofficial and invisible to upstairs.

So what does personalization of the master script involve based on the team leaders' accounts?

Field Note Entry 4.6 Changes to the typed master script allowed downstairs

Following a number of crisis meetings after an important client sent back leads, I asked Jenny whether we could not simply add a number of questions to the master script to ensure that agents asked them and the leads were indeed leads. It had emerged that agents did not ask any follow-up questions as "they were not on the script." Jenny replied that we can't do that as the script came from the client and upstairs, we can't change it. Moreover, the client has not paid for those questions. Instead, she suggested to me that I write those additional questions on a separate handout, which I could print and distribute to give to agents. I did as she told me.

Personalisation of the master script

The team leaders still work the lines, and they all said they pursued their own individual strategies for making a script their own. During the briefing, they share those strategies with the agents and act out different versions of the master script. Here are examples that Siiri, Stuart, and Ada used to show what personalization involves for them (see also Woydack and Rampton 2016).

Siiri explained to me how she writes her own script on a blank piece of paper by hand.

Extract 4.20

So it's not about changing the script, I think it's more about using the key elements in the script and making it sound like you (…). I rewrite it. I write it into one blank piece of paper from the beginning (…) so I just rewrite it and make it my own, yeah. So that's why I think it's better to have it as a guideline but just to make it sound like yourself, so it comes out of your mouth. (…) I mean the scripts are good but they sound like someone else, that…, they sound like very general kind, I think that's the problem that I faced in the beginning (…). Whatever you write down, just make it sound like you're interested. You have to be interested, you have to, you have to sell it yourself. (*Siiri, substitute team leader*)

Ada mentions "reshuffling the words" to make it sound like her:

Extract 4.21

When I say the same thing over and over again it gives me a headache (…). So I have to like reshuffle my words. I always like changing it because it's like sometimes I believe I sound like a scratched CD (…) saying the same thing over and over and over. It became so bad I was actually saying it in my sleep (…) and it wasn't even fun anymore. So you just need to change it around a bit. (*Ada, senior team leader*)

Finally, Stuart makes the changes in his head that he needs to personalize the script:

Extract 4.22

When someone brief[ed] me when I first came here; you just want to look like you're doing something to the script if they're going through and saying, "You should really underline this bit," but I don't touch scripts like that, I do it all in [my] head and verbal and just… I see what's on the page and after a few calls I know what needs to be said and what doesn't. (…) I guess there's phrases I steer clear of like *report*, not a big fan of that sort of word, because I think it's too client-driven. I use *we* a lot (…). It's odd because I always say I'm calling "on behalf of" and then I say… later on I'll drop in, "Yeah, we've just put this together," but I do it very casually so it sounds… even though I say I'm calling "on behalf of" it then sounds like I'm part of… they can't picture me, say, in a call center calling them. (*Stuart, senior team leader*)

In view of these differences in their approaches, personalization strategies are likely to have different impacts on the master script. For Siiri, it involves both hand- written and oral changes, while Stuart and Ada only talk of oral ones.

When it comes to training the agents, team leaders advise them to make any changes prior to calling. Although everyone is allowed to make hand-written changes to the script even after they have started calling, making the script one's own before they start provides an opportunity for agents to familiarize themselves with the new text. After a few calls and feedback, more hand-written notes may be added to the script and as a result, agents' personal versions are also likely to change over time.

All scripts, no matter which campaign type was involved, needed to be personalized. The same does not apply to the consultative approach. What does being consultative involve, and how are agents trained in this?

Being "consultative" with the master script

Whereas personalization centers on agents' individual preferences and needs, the consultative approach centers on the person who receives the call. Stuart, who is considered the expert in the call center on consultative calling, describes it the following way:

Extract 4.23

> The sort of consultative approach on things. (…) It's far more about them than it is about us. I find with engagement [scripts] it's all about us really, really we're calling for us. I think with engagement [campaigns], we have objectives obviously, we are getting them these things because we're employed by a company to hit them with it, but [the consultative approach is] just far more focused around them (…). (*Stuart, senior team leader*)

According to the team leaders, agents should ask a range of questions to prompt a conversation in BANT campaigns and, especially, in nurturing campaigns. Agents can do this by enquiring about the other persons' needs and asking questions like "what problems have you got at the moment?"

Extract 4.24

> The consultative approach (…) it's not ((sighs)). "We have this, take it, and then someone's going to give you a call back in the next two weeks." It's much more like, "What problems have you got at the moment? What issues are you having?" It's far more about them than it is about us. And in terms of a caller, the skills now I think that are going to be prized above any other is the consultative approach. (…) We need guys that can sit on the

phone for a quarter of an hour, 20 minutes. It's going to be far more knowledge based, for the agent. (...). It's (...) far more just talking, just having a conversation, an actual conversation. (*Stuart, team leader*)

Such conversation-prompting questions are listed on a specific training sheet. The agent is free either to integrate them into the eight sections of the already personalized master script, or to ask them after the script's basic elements have been covered. In fact, while BANT, nurturing, and engagement campaigns all have the same basic eight elements, a major difference among the campaign scripts is the number of profiling questions that follow the basic sections. Engagements usually have none, BANT some, and nurturing many (Figure 4.4).

Stuart also suggests that there are three different components of every call: tone, flow, and content.

For BANT (Budget Authority Need Time) campaigns we are looking for IT professionals who have a project due within a specific timeframe, who have the relevant authority to adjust IT parameters of the project, who can articulate specific needs for enhancing their work, and frequently those who have the authority to allocate resources from the budget.

Unlike for engagement campaigns, for BANT and for nurturing campaigns, it is often necessary to go beyond the script to clarify whether there is actually a project ongoing in their firm for which they have some responsibility. We call this a "consultative approach." It often helps to find out the answer to *why* they have a project so that we can be sure that they really have a project. In order to so do it is often good to obtain an answer to the following questions during a conversation:

Do they face any issues or problems in the respective areas? (What is their need?)

Do they have contracts/licenses which expire? Do they want to upgrade their products?

What does it depend on whether they will have the project (the budget, timeframe etc.)?

Do they have annual reviews for the relevant areas?

Fig. 4.4 Internal training document for the consultative approach

Extract 4.25

Regardless of what the information is, I think it has to be put in an engaging way. (…) change words, get rid of like whole sentences, and I'll change sentences, and I'll lynchpin it around the information that matters, that we have to let them know what it's about, but I'll change… but I'll never do the same every time. For example, if I call someone up, I probably have a phone voice. A lot of people tend to. But then if I go through to IT managers (…) if they make it much more friendly and a much more conversational thing then I will obviously mirror that in terms of I'll probably let my natural accent come through a little bit more, I won't use as formal terms I suppose (…) But I just mirror really, that's what I tend to do (…). You should let them dictate the tone. (…) You should always dictate where it [conversation] is going but let them dictate the tone and the terms they want to talk to you on. (*Stuart, senior team leader*)

While he lets the other person dictate the tone of the conversation, his control over the flow of the conversation will supposedly enable him to stay within the skeleton of the master script. For an agent to respond to the interlocutor's tone and maintain flow, listening becomes important. In fact, all the team leaders identify this as key:

Extract 4.26

I'd probably say it's the key skill, listening. (…) I don't mean just listening to what they're saying. (…) I don't know whether that comes from me being an actor but when you're on stage and when you're performing, for me the most important thing is listening, but not listening with your ears, listening with your whole body. That's what we're meant to do on stage as an actor, okay. So that doesn't just mean watching what the person's saying and waiting for your bit. You have to listen: like you say you have to have an emotional intelligence, you have to be switched on to certain movements and things. Now we don't have that on the phone but what we do have is a whole wealth of stuff that they can give us. Hence a guy saying, "Yeah, what is it?" or a guy going, "Oh all right, yeah, yeah, I'm okay." [groans] (…) You have to have a sense of being able to listen to how they are as a person. And of course it's split-second, you don't have time to sit there and get to know them, but I think listening is a massive important skill and not just to what they're saying but how they're saying it. That's all we have. But I think being adaptable, listening to them, and being able to adapt to what they're saying (...). (*Stuart, senior team leader*)

Extract 4.27

When you sense the tone of the voice of the other person who is on the other side of the line and like how to talk to people, yeah, and it's just sensing things. (...) Every single phone call is different (...). (*Piia, former team leader*)

Ada adds that it is also about listening to which things and pointers the client might find useful:

Extract 4.28

[For the consultative approach] you should be a good listener, you should be a very good listener to be honest, because at the end of the day you can put something, other pointers in the remarks, things that the client, information that the client might find very useful. (*Ada, senior team leader*)

Two different forms of writing need to go along with the consultative approach. First of all, agents are expected to take notes from call conversations on their notepad. They can then type up and save this information in the call center's database so it can be analyzed by campaign managers and subsequently passed on to the client. Second, agents are also encouraged to listen and note on their scripts any key word that seems to lead people to open up. During the briefing the team leaders will likely give agents some tips based on their experience as to what the key words and prompters for conversations could be. Agents then scribble these on their master scripts.

On the whole, the consultative approach is seen as being much less a matter of set rules. It is often described as developing a feel for the master script, the call protocol, and the other speaker. Team leaders call it developing an "intuition" (Stuart) or "sensing things" (Piia and Siiri). Ideally the other person on the phone cannot tell the agents are working from a script but rather has a sense of spontaneous conversation.

Role plays are considered useful for training agents in the consultative approach. For instance, Barbara says:

Extract 4.29

> I think that a better way to do this [to train them on the consultative approach] is to train them on the generic script but then do some role plays with them and show them how it [the script] could be modified (…). They kind of just have [to learn] to get into that role and just do it naturally, the script is not there, it just comes naturally to them. I think more role playing (…) in terms of what they might say and how they might speak might help. (*Barbara, substitute team leader*)

So in terms of standardization, we can say that although team leaders claim to follow "the standard" (master) script, this does not imply strict fidelity to the text as requested by the client. For them, following the standard means that they have a structure that allows some leeway, and this includes practical adaptations of the master script (oral or handwritten) that do not undermine or compromise the framing of that document as an authoritative reference point (cf. Bauman 1996). The master script and the notion of standardization, therefore, mean different things to team leaders and upstairs. Team leaders are pragmatic in their orientation and adaptation of the master script. They believe communication will be most successful when they personalize and adapt the script into a dialogue in which the caller reacts to their partner on the phone. Concerning the transformations that the master script undergoes at this stage, team leaders and agents hand-annotate their typed copies. Based on the discussion of the two briefings, the following characterizations can be made about the use of scripts and their potential transformations (Table 4.1).

Table 4.1 Types of scripts and their expected transformations

Type of campaign	Hand-written and oral transformations	Personalization	Consultative approach
Engagement campaigns	It can be read word for word. A few hand-written or oral transformations	Yes	No
BANT campaigns	The master script may require some oral or hand- written transformations	Yes	Yes—follow-up questions added to the master script that are context dependent, not scripted, and are based on what the other person on the phone has told them.
Nurturing campaigns	The master script will require a lot of hand-written and oral transformations.	Yes	Yes—improvise by adding a lot of questions to the master script. These questions will be context dependent and not scripted.

In the next section, I analyze concrete examples of team leaders' personalizations of scripts in order to show what personalization entails in terms of changes to the script. These examples emerged during interview role play.

Personalizing the master script in interview role play

During the interviews, I asked three of the team leaders to enact their own personalization of the pitch for BIS, the longer of the two campaign-specific sections of the script. To analyze these examples, I draw on a framework that Johnstone (2003) developed for examining individual variation in telephone interviewers' scripted speech. In line with her approach, I address two questions. First, can we observe any variation from speaker to speaker? Second, what are the continua along which team leaders' choices, overall, appear to vary? (cf. Johnstone 2003, 274).

The answer to the first question is yes, there is variation from speaker to speaker. None of the three enacted versions are the same and all vary from the master script. The two introductory sentences of the pitch illustrate this well. On the typed master script, the two introductory sentences are as follows:

> The reason for my call today is that BIS, has put together a complimentary report on SBP. The SBP is the bedrock of any organisation's management of employee use of corporate IT systems.

Figure 4.5 presents Ada's personalization of the first two sentences Specifically, we see that Ada:

S.1

- adds a "now" in the beginning
- adds a relative clause after AUP "which, as you know"

S.2

- leaves out the entire second sentence

Siiri's version of the master script looks like this:
We can observe the following changes in her personalisation:

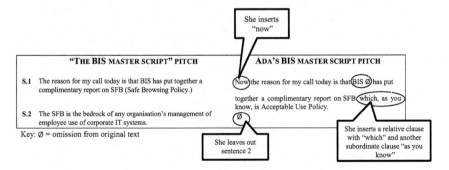

Fig. 4.5 Ada's version of the S.1–2 of the master script's pitch

Fig. 4.6 Siiri's version of S.1–2 of the master script's pitch

S.1

– she changes "has" to "have"

S.2

– she leaves out the entire second sentence

Finally, Barbara provided me with this personalisation of the first two lines:

Barbara made a range of changes:

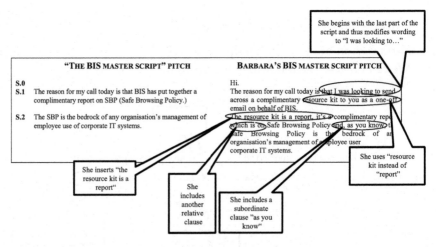

Fig. 4.7 Barbara's version of S.1–2 of the master script's pitch

S.1

- she begins with a greeting "Hi"
- she moves the purpose of the call from the end of the script to S.1 and modifies the wording to "I was looking to send across a complimentary resource kit to you"
- she uses "resource kit" instead of "report"
- she inserts "one-off email," "on behalf of" and "which is now known as X"(relative clause).

S.2

- the remaining left out information from S.1 in the master script is integrated into the second sentence
- she clarifies that the "resource kit" (her term) is a "complimentary report" (the script's term)
- she includes "which is on Acceptable Use Policy" and "as you you know"

Importantly, the three introductions all differ from one another and from the script. In their personalizations, team leaders reorder and leave out information from the script. Although these sentences vary, if one looks at the three personalized pitches and the variation as a whole below (Figures 4.8, 4.9 and 4.10), it becomes evident that from Sentence 5 (S.5), "the conclusion of the pitch," all three versions deviate significantly from the master script. Information is left out and reordered, new information is added, and entire sentences are reformulated.

These variations lead to the question, are there continua along which the utterances vary? To address this, I draw on Johnstone's framework. Johnstone gave telephone interviewers a completely scripted introduction to read. She then focused on how they changed it. The script printed for the interviewer was the following:

Hello, this___ is calling for the Texas Poll, a statewide, non-partisan public opinion poll. This month we are conducting a confidential survey of public opinion in Texas, and we'd really appreciate your help and cooperation. (quoted in Johnstone 2003, 274)

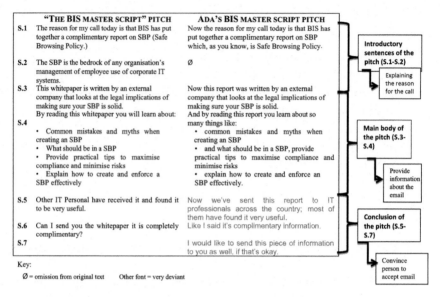

Fig. 4.8 The BIS master script pitch and Ada's personalization

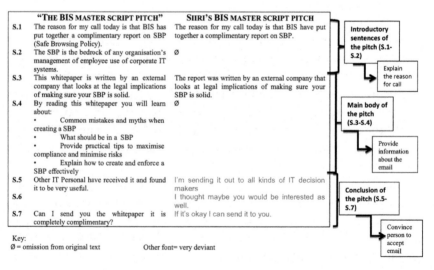

Fig. 4.9 The BIS master script pitch and Siiri's personalization

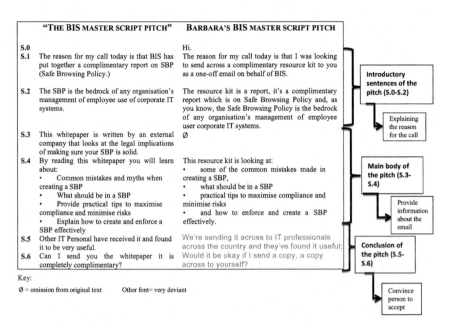

Fig. 4.10   The BIS master script pitch and Barbara's personalization

Johnstone (2003, 275) found that interviewers varied in their use of the script along two continua: discourse-syntactic and interactional. *Discourse-syntactic* refers to how the five separate clauses of the script are connected. Regarding this, the author observed that the interviewers preferred speaking a version of the script "in which bits of information were less tightly packed into clauses and more explicitly linked" to one another. They modified the original in a variety of ways (2003, 276). In the original script, there are only three independent clauses: "This is___, we are conducting a confidential survey of public opinion in Texas, we'd really appreciate your help and cooperation" (cf. Johnstone 1996, 116). Several agents used *and* as a connector between the second and third clauses (cf. Johnstone 2003, 276). Overall, they preferred more co-coordinative ways of connecting clauses to subordinate clauses. The third clause, an appositive noun phrase ("a statewide, nonpartisan public opinion poll"), was also changed by the majority of the interviewers to a finite clause. They used seven options to do so:

It's a statewide…
It's just a statewide…
This is a statewide…
This is merely a statewide…
We're a statewide…
We're doing the statewide…
which is a statewide…. (quoted from Johnstone 2003, 275)

Johnstone calls the other axis interactional (personability) (1996, 116–117; 2003, 274). This continuum describes how frequently and in which ways the agents refer to the people to whom they were talking and how they refer to themselves. In her study, she found that agents included additional personal pronouns such as *we* and *I* in the script. For instance, Elaine, one of the interviewers, inserted two necessary *we*'s and three extra first-person pronouns:

Hi, **my name** is Elaine, and **I'm** calling for the Texas Poll. **We're** a state-wide, non-partisan public opinion poll. And this month **we are** conducting a confidential survey of public opinions in Texas. **We'd** really appreciate your help and cooperation. Do you have a few moments? (quoted from Johnstone 2003: 276)

Some interviewers included *ma'am* or *sir*. Others changed the greeting from *hello* to a more "personable" *hi*, while others used the more formal *good afternoon* (Johnstone 1996, 116).

Johnstone's two continua also apply to the team leaders' personalizations at CallCentral. The interactional or *personability axis* features strongly in all three versions (marked in bold in Figures 4.11, 4.12 and 4.13 below).

In two of the versions (Figures 4.11 and 4.13), the pronoun *we* is introduced into the script. In the master script, there is no mention of *we* since agents are calling on behalf of the client. Also, team leaders complement their version with a range of personal pronouns *I, you, yourself* in each of their versions. This is summarized in Table 4.2.

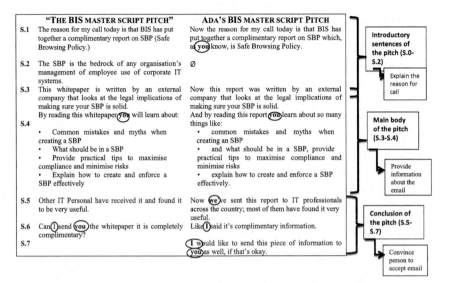

Fig. 4.11 The BIS master script pitch and Ada's inclusion of pronouns

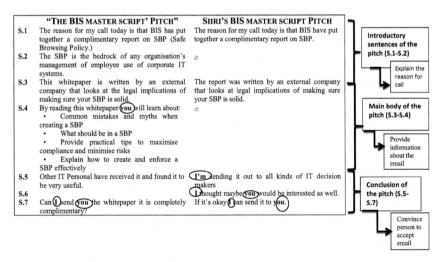

Fig. 4.12 The BIS master script pitch and Siiri's inclusion of pronouns

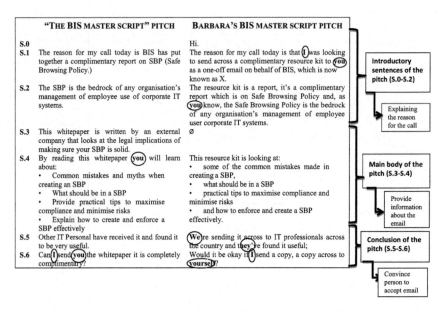

Fig. 4.13 The BIS master script pitch and Barbara's inclusion of pronouns

Table 4.2 The use of personal pronouns (personability axis)

Master script	Ada	Siiri	Barbara
1× *I* (in S.6) 2× *you* (in S.4 and S.6)	2× *I* (in S. 6 and S.7) 3× *you* (in S. 1, S. 4 and S.7) 1× *we* (in S.5)	3× *I* (in S.5, S.6 and S.7) 2× *you* (in S.6 and S.7) –	2× *I* (in S.1) 2× *you* (in S.1, S.2) 1× *we* (in S.5) 1× *they* (in S.5) 1×*yourself* (in S.6)
Total: 3	Total: 6	Total: 5	Total: 7

The majority of these pronouns are used in the concluding section, both in the master script and in the personalized versions. Below, I explore why. However, let us first look at the other discourse-syntactic continuum.

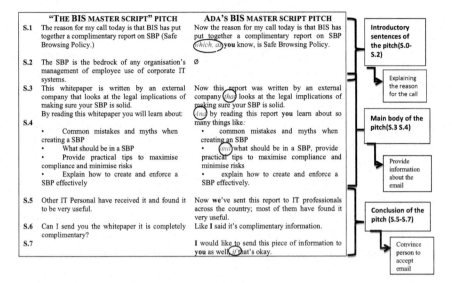

Fig. 4.14 The BIS master script pitch and Ada's inclusion of sub- and coordinate clauses

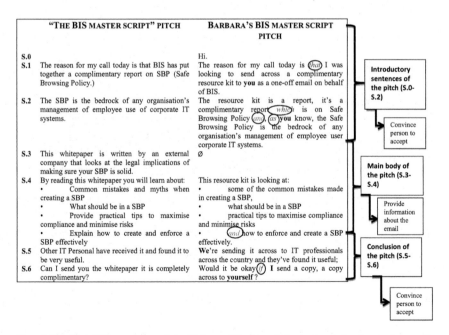

Fig. 4.15 The BIS master script pitch and Barbara's inclusion of sub- and coordinate clauses

Out of the three team leaders, Ada and Barbara are like Johnstone's informants, using subordinate and coordinate clauses to make the pitch easier to read and less dense. In Figures 4.14 and 4.15, I have highlighted in italics the subordinate or coordinate conjunctions in their speech.

These examples show that the "conclusion of the pitch" is the most deviant section of the entire script in terms of agents' predilection for changing the word order and adding new information. Additionally, many personal pronouns are included in the transformation process. Why is this the case?

The clue to this lies in the function of the pitch conclusion. Its purpose is to convince the other person to accept an email and provide further information. For this reason, in the call center this final part of the pitch (S.5–S.7) is considered separate, and team leaders and agents are allowed to change these lines freely to be as convincing as possible. Agents are even taught specific strategies for achieving this. The team leaders made the following alterations to "their conclusions" (see Figures 4.16–4.18).

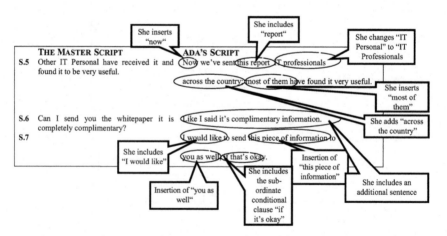

Fig. 4.16 Ada's personalization of the pitch's conclusion

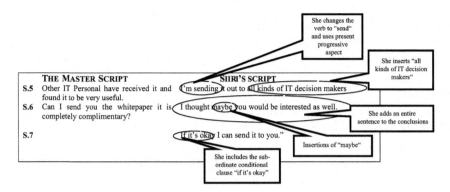

Fig. 4.17   Siiri's personalization of the pitch's conclusion

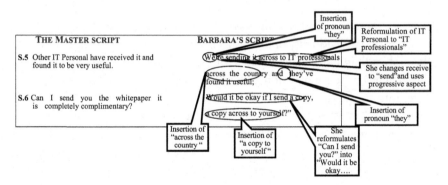

Fig. 4.18   Barbara's personalization of the pitch's conclusion

So what are the strategies behind these alterations?

The writers of the original master script used what is known in the call center as an "inclusive approach" for the concluding section of the pitch (S.5–7). That is, the last two sentences stress the global appeal of the resource and how even important people apparently have accepted it and "found it useful." The approach is also meant to make the action of accepting the resource over the phone from an unknown agent less threatening and risky. The "fact" that so many other people have already taken the email is intended to convince the person on the phone to do the same.

The three team leaders align with this inclusive strategy of the master script by keeping the gist of this part of the message. In addition, they use other approaches. One appears to make the original pitch more polite by using *would*, and by using hedges such as *maybe*. Second, they exaggerate certain parts of the message. So it is not only *IT Personnel* (master script) who have received the email but "IT professionals across the country" (Barbara) or "all kinds of IT decision makers" (Siiri). Finally, downstairs it is considered vital to establish rapport with the person on the phone, especially in the concluding part of the pitch. One way to do this is to insert personal pronouns to make the call not only relevant to the person addressed but to reach out to them on a personal level.

These three examples suggest two axes dominate personalization strategies: interactional and discourse-syntactic. Moreover, as Johnstone (2003, 280) suggests, these changes make the script "easier to understand by ear" and they enhance "the individuality of the speaker." That is, the callers sound more like themselves than like a representative of the company. As I explained earlier, the strategy of "personalization" allows the caller to insert his/her own preferences into the framework of the script. A listener on the other end of the call then "hears" an earnest message, not a rote advertisement.

At the same time, team leader Siiri leaves out the key points of the main body of the master pitch in her enactment. She is the least experienced of all the team leaders and that may explain her *faux pas*. She was made temporary team leader after only four weeks at the call center, at a time of such great need that her inexperience was overlooked. Her lack of experience may also account for the fact that she applies fewer "personalization strategies" to the script than her colleagues. The campaign managers would be unhappy with her enactment and would reprimand her. The question of whether the client's needs are compromised when team leaders and agents personalize the master script emerges in light of Siiri's choices. Upstairs would probably say that the clients' needs are compromised without full textual fidelity. Downstairs believes that the interest of the client is served if the call is memorable, personalized, and the key information is conveyed in a variety of ways. Although it is beyond the scope of this book to answer this question, clearly upstairs and downstairs have different motivations for their positions, but both are convinced they are acting in the interest of the company and the client.

At this point it is clear that scripts, and by extension standardization, mean different things to the participants as we descend the organization's hierarchy, reflecting their divergent orientations. At the top level of the organization, the management "upstairs" has what seems a rather "purist" view of scripts and standardization. They implement a number of measures internally, such as requiring agents or leaders to read scripts word for word or acquiring regulatory statistics to meet a client's demands for transparency. Conversely, the management downstairs, including the team leaders, have a more pragmatic view of scripts and standardization. They understand a script to be a kind of "skeleton" or "scaffolding" that provides a structure to follow, a structure required for regulatory purposes. At the same time, they allow flexibility and require improvisation on the structure in the form of hand-written personal notes. On the whole, while upstairs is opposed to any written or oral changes on the script sold to the client, downstairs is not. In sum, differences in the meaning of the script and of standardization are manifested in i) the different orientations participants display toward the script across the different activities and stages of its career and ii) the resulting transformations that it undergoes. At a more general level, these transformations in the text and the different orientations show that the literature's view of standardization as a homogenous concept is too simple.

If we think back to the theory of transposition and the advantage of following textual trajectories as modes of analysis, Figures 4.5, 4.6, 4.7, 4.8, 4.9, 4.10, 4.11, 4.12, 4.13, 4.14, 4.15, 4.16, 4.17 and 4.18 are evidence of team leaders' agency in transforming the master script. The analysis also reveals what motivated the leaders to transform the text. Team leaders, even Siiri, are not adapting the script to perform acts of resistance, but to comply with what they have learned downstairs.

Conclusion: campaign managers and team leaders negotiating between upstairs and downstairs

As the master script moves downstairs, senior call center staff receive it with skepticism of corporate management's "purist" stance. These campaign managers and team leaders try to redirect the push for monitoring. They recognize that campaign targets and verbatim reproduction are often at odds. And with more junior staff they are explicit about the need to personalize a script. The eight-section approach used downstairs is a practical framework to cope with the sheer volume of multilingual calls and the number of languages that need monitoring since it shifts the focus from literal word-to-word translations to the more abstract eight sections.

CallCentral campaign managers and team leaders are aware of the commercial calculations that underpin the script. They respect its basic structure and recognize that each segment has an important purpose. For example, the closing phrase used to compete a call (Figure 3.2) is required for legal reasons. But they also think of the script as a skeleton to be transposed in details, fleshed out, or adjusted according to the situational and, in the case of translations, the cultural context.

I have suggested that standardization is not a homogenous process and does not mean the same thing to different people in the organization. For the team leaders, following the standard of the script does not mean complete textual fidelity. In fact, they believe there is leeway for adaptation to maximize a caller's connection with their counterpart on the phone without compromising the authority of the script. We have also seen that although upstairs sometimes finds out that downstairs does not follow the script verbatim, most of the time campaign managers manage the gap systematically and mediate between the different parties, for example, by advising agents on how to rewrite their script while also confirming to management that scripts are followed.

We saw in the first chapter that the majority of the few studies on organizational resistance and control take either a neo-Marxist or a Foucauldian approach. Notwithstanding the vast epistemological divide between the two, these analyses have been criticized for framing resistance as juxtaposed with control, and they rarely go beyond this. For example, Mumby laments that both Foucauldian and neo-Marxian scholars address resistance in individual terms. Latent at best is any notion of collective workers' struggles or consciousness. Attention to an "onward, irresistible march of managerialism" tends to silence the collective impact of workers (Mumby 2005, 27). Similar to the broader literature on workplace resistance, Leidner writes that sociologists addressing standardization have also preferred to focus on instances of open individual resistance to control (1993, 5).

In call center studies, Foucauldian-inspired analyses are prevalent. Most researchers have argued that the panoptic control achieved through technological advances leaves no possibility for collective action and little room for individual resistance. From this perspective, team leaders and agents are complicit in the creation of their own discipline (cf. e.g., Fernie and Metcalf 1998; Knights and McCabe 1998). Following this argument, the fact that managers and supervisors have access to real-time statistics comprising every keystroke and action agents ever carry out, and that they can listen to any call without prior warning, establishes "the ultimate surveillance regime" (McPhail 2002, 44). Moreover, the rigorous top-down enforcement of management's decisions supports this position. Illustrative of this is Fernie and Metcalf's widely quoted assertion that "the tyranny of the assembly line is but a Sunday school picnic compared with the control that management can exercise in computer telephony" (1998, 2). Downstairs is perceived as having little choice but to comply with regulations, including linguistic ones that entail following a script that is codified to the smallest detail. Studies such as those by Cameron (Cameron 2000, 2008), Mirchandani (2004), and Taylor and Tyler (2000) assume that workers must be discontented if they have to follow a script and work within managers' attempts to control their speech. These scholars sometimes hunt painstakingly for instances of agents resisting the script and beating the system. For example, Cameron notes:

> Tyler and Taylor (1997 cited in Cameron 2000) found telephone sales and reservations staff at an airline company insisting that they could tell when they were being monitored. These reported that if they encountered a rude or "ignorant" caller and were sure no one was listening in, they would deviate from the prescribed routine, and might even disconnect the offender (2000, 99). (…) My informants reported taking liberties with their scripts and ignoring instructions to smile. (2000, 113)

For Cameron, the symbol of control is the script and thus the obvious site for collective resistance. But she implies and assumes that any such action, heroic as it is, will be in vain because of the individualistic focus of the extensive monitoring.

Although team leaders adapt the script, it is clear that the adaptations do not constitute resistance. The team leaders, with the exception of Stuart, are unaware of upstairs' stress on textual fidelity. Also with the exception of Stuart (because he is the team leader for high-end nurturing campaigns), team leaders do not have any interaction with upstairs beyond the campaign managers. During their training and briefings, campaign managers instruct them on how to adapt the script by hand. These instructions entail keeping the meaning (the key points and eight sections) and the topic constant during implementation. For the adaptations to be "resistance," team leaders would have to defy the eight-section framework or the general structure of the script. During the interviews, team leaders explained that they welcomed the use of scripts and were keen to follow them. They referred to the script as the "standard" and emphasized the importance of mentioning "the key points" when training their agents. More importantly, they appeared to make a great effort with their adaptations, revealing a desire to do their jobs well and to make significant connections with customers. This good faith behind the processes of transposition reflects the investment team leaders have in their company. Their script adaptations are intended to help the business succeed. Their actions are taken in the best interest of their company and in the belief that they are enacting the client's directives, and are not steps to undermine call labor or to sabotage the larger industry.

We have seen how the script changes when team leaders adapt it. So what happens when the master script is appropriated by the agents who actually make the calls?

References

Bauman, Richard. 1996. Transformations of the Word in the Production of Mexican Festival Drama. In *Natural Histories of Discourse*, ed. Michael Silverstein and Greg Urban, 301–329. Chicago/London: Chicago University Press.

Cameron, Deborah. 2000. *Good to Talk?* London: Sage.

———. 2008. Talk from the Top Down. *Language & Communication* 28 (2): 143–155.

Fernie, Sue, and David Metcalf. 1998. *(Not) Hanging on the Telephone: Payment Systems in the New Sweatshops*. London: London School of Economics, Centre for Economic Performance.

Johnstone, Barbara. 1996. *The Linguistic Individual: Self-Expression in Language and Linguistics*, Oxford Studies in Sociolinguistics. New York: Oxford University Press.

———. 2003. The Linguistic Individual in an American Public Opinion Survey. In *Sociolinguistics – The Essential Readings*, ed. C.B. Paulston and R. Tucker, 272–286. Oxford: Blackwell.

Knights, David, and Darren McCabe. 1998. 'What Happens When the Phone Goes Wild?': Staff, Stress and Spaces for Escape in a BPR Telephone Banking Work Regime. *Journal of Management Studies* 35 (2): 163–194.

Leidner, Robin. 1993. *Fast Food, Fast Talk: Service Work and the Routinization of Everyday Life*. Berkeley: University of California Press.

McPhail, Brenda. 2002. *What Is 'On the Line' in Call Centre Studies? A Review of Key Issues on Academic Literature*. University of Toronto. http://www3.fis.utoronto.ca/research/iprp/publications/mcphail-cc.pdf

Mirchandani, Kiran. 2004. Practices of Global Capital: Gaps, Cracks and Ironies in Transnational Call Centres in India. *Global Networks* 4 (4): 355–373.

Mumby, Dennis K. 2005. Theorizing Resistance in Organization Studies: A Dialectical Approach. *Management Communication Quarterly* 19 (1): 19–44.

Smith, Dorothy E. 1996. The Relations of Ruling: A Feminist Inquiry. *Studies in Cultures, Organizations and Societies* 2 (2): 171–190.

Taylor, Steve, and Melissa Tyler. 2000. Emotional Labour and Sexual Difference in the Airline Industry. *Work, Employment and Society* 14 (1): 77–95.

Woydack, Johanna. 2016. Superdiversity and a London Multilingual Call Centre. In *Engaging Superdiversity: Recombining Spaces, Times and Language Practices*, ed. Karel Arnaut, Martha Sif Karrebaek, Massimiliano Spotti, and Jan Blommaert, vol. 7, 220–251. Bristol: Multilingual Matters.

Woydack, Johanna, and Ben Rampton. 2016. Text Trajectories in a Multilingual Call Centre: The Linguistic Ethnography of a Calling Script. *Language in Society* 45 (05): 709–732.

5

The Final Stage of the Script's Career: Enactment and Use of the Master Script

Introduction

In the previous chapter, we saw that a script acquires new significance the moment it travels downstairs to the call center, where it is adapted by the team leaders and agents. In this chapter, I explore the final stage in the career of a script: its initial testing and potential use by agents, also known as "callers."

Smith (1996, 177) theorized that texts function in large corporations as "mediators and base of discourse and relations of ruling that regulate and coordinate beyond the particular local setting of their reading and writing." In the case of CallCentral, upstairs management uses the master script to regulate downstairs. Even though the regulation does not happen exactly as intended, the master script plays an important role in briefings by campaign managers and team leaders. Here I begin where the last chapter ended, and explore what happens after the BIS script has been individually hand-annotated.

This phase of a script's career is important in the transpositional process. The document as annotated by leaders and management is further subject to oral and written transformations as callers tailor the message to their own style. The script is used by countless agents who rehearse the

© The Author(s) 2019
J. Woydack, *Linguistic Ethnography of a Multilingual Call Center:*
London Calling, Communicating in Professions and Organizations,
https://doi.org/10.1007/978-3-319-93323-8_5

anticipated script delivery to test their comfort with the details. It is also translated into other languages. In the call center's database, callers are supposed to record the feedback from their phone interactions using the script. The results obtained from this process then feed into the decision about whether to continue the use of the script as is or whether and how significantly to alter the script. The client and upstairs may choose to replace it with a new campaign script when results are disappointing.

In the first section, I look at callers' activities involving the script. In the second section, I examine agents' adaptations of the BIS master script in practice. Subsequently, I look at how data entry and logging, an important aspect of the production and accountability system in agents' practices on this level, affect agents' transposition of the script.

I draw on several sources in this chapter: my field notes, training documents, a recorded telephone conversation, and 33 interviews I conducted with callers. The agents I interviewed and to whose accounts I refer in this chapter are listed in Table 5.1.

We resume the story of the BIS campaign at the point where agents leave their briefing by team leaders, equipped with the script they have each hand-annotated during their meeting. They begin to make their calls.

Rehearsing and using the master script: a script in progress

In the last chapter, we saw that campaign managers and team leaders think of the master script as a structure. All the agents interviewed held a similar opinion. For instance, Roberto says,

Extract 5.1

> I think that the script is (…) just structure that we can change in the end. (…) the script is just… a form (…) so I think as long as we think about it like a form, like it would be okay if I change the script. (*Roberto, current agent*)

Table 5.1 Agents' background

Agent's name	Type of agent	Background	Types of campaign caller
Akash	Current agent	BA	Engagement BANT nurturing
Alex	Current agent	BA	Engagement BANT
Anand	Current agent	BA and MA	Engagement BANT
Andreas	Ex-agent	BA and MA	Engagement BANT
Beatrice	Current agent	BA	Engagement BANT
Charlotte	Current agent	BA	Engagement BANT
Christina	Current agent	BA and MA	Engagement BANT
Daniela	Current agent	BA	Engagement BANT
David	Current agent	BA	Engagement BANT
Ian	Ex-agent	BA	Engagement
Jonas	New agent	BA and MA	Engagement BANT
Juan	Current agent	BA and MA	Engagement BANT
Kadeem	Current agent	BA	Engagement
Linda	Current agent	BA, MA and PhD	Engagement
Linnea	Current agent	BA and MA	Engagement BANT
Marta	Ex-agent	BA and MA	Engagement BANT
Michael	New agent	BA and MA	Engagement
Miguel	Current agent	BA	Engagement BANT
Paulina	Current agent	BA	Engagement BANT
Rabeya	Current agent	BA	Engagement BANT
Raul	Current agent	BA	Engagement BANT
Roberto	Current agent	BA and MA	Engagement BANT
Stephen	New agent	–	Engagement
Sonia	Current agent	BA student	Engagement BANT
Suganthi	Current agent	BA	Engagement BANT
Suhela	Current agent	BA	Engagement BANT
Tina	Ex-agent	BA, MA, PhD	Engagement BANT
Tom	New agent	BA student	Engagement
Vanessa	New agent	BA	Engagement BANT
Yannick	Current agent	BA, MA	Engagement BANT nurturing
Yasmin	New agent	BA	Engagement BANT

But what does this mean when callers start using the master script on the phone? Do they also personalize the master script and use the consultative approach the team leaders taught them?

Step 6: Before Dialing: Translating the master script

Campaigns such as the anonymized BIS model campaign are typically aimed at firms in the UK and at businesses in other countries, such as Germany and France. The master script thus needs to be translated. But because of the cost involved in hiring external professional translators, the call center usually asks agents already on the payroll to perform this task. Depending on the circumstances of the campaigns and the timing within the quarter, they may do this as a group or on their own. Occasionally, a client may also ask to see the translated script(s), but they do not adjust the translation. They trust the call center with this.

However, as the vignette below reveals, certain problems may arise when callers translate the master script as shown in Field note entry 5.1.

It is not unusual that translation would involve issues such as these and indeed, concerns associated with cultural norms and technical issues were often mentioned by the agents I interviewed.

For example, Yasmin commented on the importance of knowing the cultural norms of the target market when translating a script:

Extract 5.2

> You cannot translate literally because from one language to another (…) It really depend [sic] on the market. I mean French market you have to be formal. You have to start with "Mr…" and cannot say "Hi, Hi Peter, how are you today?" In the British market it's different because they are informal. (…) I think it's very important to take into consideration the culture as well…because if I do the same thing in France, "Hi Peter," they'll ask me, "Do I know you?" (*Yasmin, new agent*)

Many also mentioned the difficulty of translating specific terms from English into other languages. For instance, Yannick describes how he initially struggled with translating technical terms into his native French:

Extract 5.3

> It was very difficult when I started because I never actually worked… or a long time ago, 15 years ago I worked in French but I've always done that [worked] in English, so my technical knowledge is stronger in English than it is in French (…)." (*Yannick, current agent*) (Source: Woydack 2016)

David reports a similar experience with his Portuguese:

Field Note Entry 5.1 Translating master scripts

Around twenty new callers were hired for a new campaign. The campaign was supposed to run in twenty different markets. Thus, nineteen scripts had to be translated into into French, Italian, Russian, Spanish, Norwegian, Finnish, Turkish, Swedish, German, Czech, Portuguese, Serbo- Croatian, Hebrew, Danish, Dutch, Polish, Slovenian, Greek and Arabic. Every agent was given a script template [with the script's eight sections] and nineteen of the agents were to be given copies of the script and then each of them asked to translate the English master script into a language of their expertise. Once they had done so, it would be printed for them. However, the issue was that agents did not necessarily know how to translate the master script with its complex IT vocabulary. For instance, there was a Somali agent who had lived for some time in Norway and was supposed to translate a script into Norwegian as a native speaker. But he told me that he could not to translate the script as he did not know the vocabulary. His solution was to use Google Translator and copy and paste the different sentences into the template. But in the past, there had been many complaints about agents who had done this. Other agents said that the translations were so poor that they had to re-translate the entire script, which also raised the issue of how agents who clearly did not speak the language could make any translations.

The new German agent equally struggled. He told me, in German, he had no idea how to translate words like "network convergence" or "network integrity." Additionally, he was also rather upset that he was even asked to do this. In his words, he was not hired for this and that they should pay a language agency for this. My response was to tell him to try his best.

A Polish girl who knew some Russian also struggled with translating a script into Russian. She was rather afraid to translate the script telling me that she did not know the language that well nor was she sure of how to translate the cultural norms and politeness formulas.

In the meanwhile, Jenny asked me why everyone was taking so long. I told her that several agents were struggling with translating the technical vocabulary. She looked at me angrily and pointed out that all the new callers are native speakers hired through language agencies. [They charge the call center a premium for having tested the agent's proficiency beforehand]. Thus, there should not be any problem. Twenty minutes later, the German agent still had no idea how to translate the script. I told him not to worry, that I would make the translation for him.

In fact, when needed I had translated scripts from English into Italian, German, Spanish and French. I found this often frustrating as I did not know the correct technical terminology or jargon in all those languages. Every time I translated a script I spent time searching the web for technical terms or collocations. Whether the phrases I came up with are actually used in those languages, I never knew. I was, of course, aware that my translations could not take into account many cultural norms. (Adapted from Woydack and Rampton 2016)

Extract 5.4

My Portuguese is not technical (…) I learnt to speak Portuguese at home with my family and friends. So when I translate or I'm calling the IT Managers I don't know the words for like IT or system and all of these I just try my best to get my point across. (*David, current agent*) (Source: Woydack 2016)

Several callers further note that they are uncertain whether the technical terms have to be translated. For example, Linda says that in German, the English technical terms are often kept.

Extract 5.5

One needs to be really careful with technical terms [in German], sometimes you don't translate those. This has happened to me a couple of times [that she tried to translate them] and was rather embarrassing. (*Linda, current agent*) (Source: Woydack 2016)

Conversely, Juan points out that in Spanish there is usually an equivalent.

Extract 5.6

[When you] translate you [have] to interpret what that's [sic] means in your language. (…) Sometimes it takes some pieces of English, but mainly in Spanish because (…) in my language they (…) adapt every single word [even technical terms] to the language (…) every single word have [has] a Spanish interpretation. (*Juan, current agent*)

As indicated in the vignette, agents do not necessarily translate into what they would call their "native language." For instance, Carolina, who belongs to a Swedish minority in Finland, told me that she had never translated into her native language:

Extract 5.7

I was given a script in English and I had to [translate] the script in Norwegian (…). Norwegian is not my mother tongue and but (…) still I had to do it in Norwegian which I found a bit frustrating. (…) I have never been given a script in Swedish (…). (*Carolina, current agent*) (Source: Woydack 2016)

Considering this context, it is perhaps not surprising that some callers said that they often have to re-translate the already translated scripts. So Vanessa says,

Extract 5.8

With the BIS script I found the translation very poor. It looked like it was done with Google translator so we as a team sat together and started reformulating it. (*Vanessa, current agent*) (Source: Woydack 2016)

Miguel adds that sometimes the translations are not "accurate" or good for use on the phone.

Extract 5.9

Sometimes the translation is not so accurate (…). Sometimes it has to do with how it's going to sound. So if it's going to sound too artificial you change it with words that make sense, makes things like easier for the people who are listening (…). You want your call to sound like speech, not a script…and there's a difference between speech and script. So you can read a script but you can't read speech, you need to create your own speech, so (…) I think it's logical to change something. (*Miguel, current agent*)

The call center management and upstairs were mostly monolingual and had no experience in translations and where the pitfalls might lie. They had no way to check whether a particular translation was good or not, or what the actual level of a speaker's competence was when hired as they did not speak the languages themselves. As a result, a script may be translated and retranslated, and transformed by various agents in the process. This is confirmed by agents like Yannick who state that through the process of translating they simultaneously personalize the master script.

Extract 5.10

> You don't translate word by word so it had to make sense, and that was not always evident. Like you extract the meaning of the speech…of the script, and then you make it your own word[s]. (*Yannick, current agent*)

Step 7: Personalizing a script and putting it to use

Apart from the context of translation, I investigated how others talk about personalizing a script and what constitutes their steps as they did so. All agents thought it natural to personalize the master script ("make it their own") before starting to use it on the phone. They adapted it as they received feedback on the phone and tried out different versions. Carolina suggested that because a script is neutral, one makes a choice about which bits to use.

Extract 5.11

> When you just look at a script it's (…) of course it is quite objective, neutral. [So] You think which words work for me or which phrases will be for me. (*Carolina, current agent*)

There is some agreement that this can done by hand, on scrap paper, in the agent's notebook, or by scribbling on the master script itself. This activity is associated with the early stages of a new campaign.

Extract 5.12

> I always underline words [in the script]; I think a lot of people do that. (*Michael, new agent*)

Extract 5.13

The first thing I do [before calling] is I will just write my own speech.
(*Rabeya, current agent*)

Extract 5.14

I would reword it [script on a spare piece of paper] (…) 'cause it's very long
sentences so that's where it gets hard to say it. (*Michael, new agent*)

Extract 5.15

[Once given a new campaign script] I changed the wording of the script.
So it was the same message but with different words but I did write down
my own script and I had it in front of me with the original script. (*Marta,
former agent*) (Source: Woydack and Rampton 2016)

Extract 5.16

I read the script and pick up the words, the key words, and then I put kind
of my words on it. (…) I interpret the script. (…) I'll rewrite the script on
a spare piece of paper. (*Miguel, current agent*)

According to Vanessa, annotating the script may also be done by a
team:

Extract 5.17

We [the team] underlined, highlighted and for some points we added some
notes or different expressions or words [on the script] one could use instead.
(*Vanessa, current agent*)

In a variety of ways, agents make changes to the wording of a master
script and contribute to its transposition. It is, however, their interpretation of how things are supposed to be personalized that is indicative of
their agency. I explore now what agents say about what happens when
they dial.

Step 8: Experimenting with the master script: in search of the perfect version

Most agents agree that their rewritten script is not necessarily the "perfect script," so one needs to try out different versions. As Kadeem says,

Extract 5.18

I change it [the script] a little bit just to see what the reaction is (…). So I'll get sort of like in a way feedback. So if they understand it fully or they want me to explain again, I'll just change a few things around. I mean that's it, feedback's very important on how to improve scripts all the time. Feedback from yourself and from another person. You have to obviously get to know the reaction to it. So obviously you have to sort of like get the right script, get the pitch (…) so they understand it. (…) You could say a "work in progress." (*Kadeem, current agent*) (Adapted from Woydack and Rampton 2016)

Linda and Jonas mention doing the same, showing how the dialogic properties of interaction further shape the transposition of the master script.

Extract 5.19

I will write my own version of the script but I will also try out different versions of that script to see which version of the script and key points are received better or not so well and then I adapt my version accordingly. So I will maybe change a few words around till I find the right script. (*Linda, current agent*)

Extract 5.20

I will write my own script so that I can work with it well. But with the feedback on the phone you will notice which words trigger a positive or negative reaction, what they like. So based on that I will always try and improve my script to the point that I'll have the perfect script. (*Jonas, new agent*)

Alex even requests several copies of the master script to try out different things.

Extract 5.21

I actually ask for several copies of the [master] script and I underline different things on different scripts and try them out. (*Alex, current agent*)

Thus, as soon as agents start dialing they continue annotating their hand-written scripts or take more notes on their individually hand-annotated paper copy, incorporating the feedback they receive over the phone. In fact, only three of the 50+ agents I interviewed said that once they found the "right script," they would repeat it in every call. But these interviewees, clearly a small minority of the agents in any case, had only joined the call center recently and they had not yet participated in the consultative approach. Other callers said that, without affecting content, they would continue altering wording and emotional tone even after they had found the "right script."

Miguel, for instance, says that despite scripts' usefulness, one has to be selective in one's use of it. More importantly, one cannot just read it. One needs to interpret it and perform it to be convincing, not read it in a monotonous voice.

Extract 5.22

But the script I think is like the tiny wheels in the bicycle (...) these wheels that you put when you are learning how to ride a bicycle. (...) you need to know when to let it go, you know, the script. (...) it's even like a love letter. If you read a love letter to someone, it sounds silly, so you need to maybe read a little bit, take part of them, and then make a speech about that (...). I think scripts are good because it gives you like a base (...) like a ground where to be (...) don't go a lot like out of here [outside the boundaries]. (*Miguel, current agent*)

According to David, the pressure of high dial rates constrains him in his use of the script.

Extract 5.23

I think if the call targets were lower, if we had more time to speak to every person so you could get more in the way of (…), you're not [an agent] saying bla, bla, next call bla, bla, but you could actually talk to them. (*David, current agent*)

Besides the pressure of high dial rates, agents' accounts pointed to a range of different influences. David and Daniela suggest that beating the monotony was one of them.

Extract 5.24

So after a while if you have been at a campaign for long enough you do find yourself just saying it and that's when I think it gets the worst as you will just be saying it monotonously. You will be just like bla, bla, but you just will be used to it not from the script but you're reading it like from your head, you will follow the same sort of pattern (…). So I do like to try to switch [it] off every so often and keep it like you're entertained and happy (…). You will have to play it around, like make a little joke with the IT Manager here and there. (*David, current agent*)

Extract 5.25

It would be too boring to always say exactly the same thing. I need a bit of change from time to time. (*Daniela, current agent*) (Adapted from Woydack and Rampton 2016)

Several agents further point out that learning from others was another factor.

Extract 5.26

If you can't get any leads you will sit listening to other people. Some people can get a lot of leads, then just listen to them (…), how they start chat with people, and you copy them (…) in your way. (*Tina, current agent*) (Adapted from Woydack and Rampton 2016)

Moreover, team leaders also like to draw on this method and place new agents next to more experienced callers who are using the script in the same language. Miguel recalled his experience sitting next to Juan, a star caller, and the impact this had on his script.

Extract 5.27

I remember that they put me next to Juan. And I remember that when I read my script for the first time I noticed that I couldn't use that, you know, as a script just to follow because it didn't sound natural. And when I was listening to him it sounded really different. So then was when I understood that I had to make my own script. I remember then I went to my house and rewrite [rewrote] my own script. And, yeah, and then I did that with all my scripts from then. (*Miguel, current agent*) (Source: Woydack 2016)

Others, like David, mention going up to the high achievers and asking them for their scripts.

Extract 5.28

I usually (…) ask [successful agents], how are you getting so many leads? What are you saying? Let me see your script! (*David, current agent*)

Sometimes during the course of the campaign there are debriefings. During these, feedback is collected regarding what seems to work and what does not. These can lead to revisions in scripts. Charlotte, for instance, says that she integrates what she hears there into her script.

Extract 5.29

During the campaign debriefings it is sometimes asked whether anyone has a trick or (…) feedback. I collected what the other people's reactions are, what sounds good or with what people engage and don't respond to and then I will integrate this into my script. (*Charlotte, current agent*)

Most callers further agree that the other person's reaction on the phone is important for any further changes to the script. David and Daniela confirm this:

Extract 5.30

I don't think that conversations, they don't go along the lines of 'I say this, you say that.' It does not work like that. So every script you have has to have some sort of leniency to if this person says this and obviously you will have to react differently and say different stuff. (*David, current agent*)

Extract 5.31

I will change my script according to their reaction. (*Daniela, current agent*)

Rabeya stresses that this may include the need to build rapport with the other person, to "mirror" them, but it is also a way to accommodate them.

Extract 5.32

I think you have to be a real friend, you have to be a people person, you have to be talkative, communicate (…), you have to speak to them as if you are speaking to a work colleague. (…) You have to be empathetic (…). It depends on the situation, who you're speaking to, their mood as well, because they might not always be the most cheerful people that you speak to and also they're really busy people, and if you just sound as if you're really hyperactive, very happy, a bit too enthusiastic, you know, that just puts them off automatically (…): you have to sound real, you have to sound very real; you can't just be smiley, smiley. (*Rabeya, current agent*)

Being creative was one way agents hoped to make their scripts unique and more interesting to listeners.

Extract 5.33

> It's about understanding the script and being able to ad lib, so just freestyling you've got to make it interesting for them (…), and… you've just got to understand it and not every one person's the same; there's not one standard format for everyone. (*Alex, current agent*)

Extract 5.34

> You have to try and make your script unique (…). You're more selling yourself. (*David, current agent*) (Source: Woydack and Rampton 2016)

According to Anand, Alex, and Jonas, one's script needs to make an impact on the other person and therefore has to be interesting.

Extract 5.35

> The thing is that you edit. You take out the important parts and I think it would vary from individual to individual. What I do is that I see what's the important thing and I, like I choose the key words which I feel are going to have an impact on the person I'm speaking to, so he might be interested and listening to me. It depends on the script, on the campaign, on the individual person how you want to change it. (*Anand, current agent*)

Extract 5.36

> But you have to be colorful with the scripts. You've got to use like the kind of poetic language that give[s] you [an edge] (…) and you've got to make it interesting. (*Alex, current agent*) (Source: Woydack and Rampton 2016)

Several agents, many among them not high-end callers, state that they draw on their cultural knowledge of the specific countries/regions they call to make the script interesting, but they are adamant that these strategies are not universal.

Extract 5.37

I think different countries need different approaches. (*Alex, current agent*)

Extract 5.38

Having seen people achieve results from all different genders, all different backgrounds, and all different ages, I think now possibly from pure practical experience, maybe it [nativeness] is not as important. (*Stuart, senior team leader*) (Source: Woydack 2016)

Extract 5.39

[Nativeness does not matter] I think it's just to do with being a natural speaker, that helps. I'm not talking about being a good public speaker because you are behind a phone, but certain people is [are] good at words, simply good at words, (…) there are so many ways to express something that sometimes you put things in such a way that sounds better and sounds more appealing. (*Miguel, current agent*)

In fact, in Chapter 2 we saw that calling scripts can help with agents' language learning. At the same time, knowledge of sociolinguistic stereotypes can be beneficial. For instance, agents note that in some cases, the script can be made interesting by saying that they are calling from London (and in English). As Miguel explains:

Extract 5.40

I think this, if you are calling to maybe in South Africa or to Asia and you are calling in English and [from] London, you are making an impact because in their social imagination to speak in English and being from the West means being sophisticated. (…). (*Miguel, current agent*)

Alex confirms that this is the case for Portugal. When he calls in Portuguese, he always mentions that he is calling from London.

Extract 5.41

You just say, "I'm calling from London," [when calling Portugal] they'll do anything. They'll transfer me to a person's house just 'cause I'm calling from London. (*Alex, current agent*) (Source: Woydack and Rampton 2016)

Similarly, Stuart comments that mentioning the location he is calling from when contacting Middle Eastern countries usually has an impact on the other person:

Extract 5.42

[When I call the Middle East and say I call from London they say] 'Ooh, this is a guy calling from England; this must be important." There's a bit of a fear there as to why they're being called. (*Stuart, team leader*)

Other callers think adding country-specific jokes to the script helps. So, Yasmin, a Belgian agent, says when phoning France she starts by making jokes about her nationality given that the French like to laugh about their neighbors. She uses this strategy to break the ice and to get the other person's attention.

Extract 5.43

[Calling France] if I see like they're so strict, I know they like to laugh about Belgium, they say you're Belgian so... because I have so many jokes about Belgians, so I will break this coldness and saying, you know, I'm from Belgium (...) [and tell them jokes about Belgians] like that's how I lead [begin my calls]. (*Yasmin, new agent*)

Piia says she adapts the script to her local dialect, taking advantage of the fact that other Finns perceive people speaking this variety as funny and relaxed.

Extract 5.44

The reason I got quite, quite easily the leads [in Finland] was because I come from East Finland, we have a funny dialect, so whenever I was pitching them I was actually pitching in my dialect from East Finland and ((laughs)) they found it really funny. They were like really listening 'cause they want to understand what I'm saying. And they were like… it's people who come from East Finland are usually really friendly and laid back and if they contact someone from West or South they're like "Wow!" (*Piia, former team leader*)

Tom believes that British people like being called by someone who sounds genuinely British.

Extract 5.45

I keep to the English accent, because I think that I've got quite a, you know, naturally reasonably well spoken accent. (…) because I'm quite like a classically middle-class person, put their hands up and say it. That's why I think it works, because they don't usually get calls from people with that kind of voice, if you know what I mean, but I think that's why it works— especially for events. Because for events it sounds like, oh wow, god, it sounds like maybe Tony Blair's invited me along or something. So, you know, it works. The Hugh Grant thing seems to pull [it] off. (*Tom, new agent*)

There is, nevertheless, a certain risk for agents trying to "sell themselves" and using the personality and accents to make the script unique. They can reveal too much about themselves and as a result be insulted or verbally abused by people on the phone. Agents seem to be aware of this, so many mention politeness as an important additional ingredient to the script to create a friendlier atmosphere for the conversation. Nonetheless, the notion of what is considered polite varies greatly among callers, illustrating the sheer number of backgrounds that can be found in the call center and the differences between countries, regions, cultures, and languages. For instance, Linda, a Swedish agent from Finland, finds people in the UK polite, whereas Roberto, an Italian, describes the British as rude.

Extract 5.46

People are really polite here compared to Scandinavian people but compared to India they (…) are rude compared to India (…). (*Linda, current agent*)

Extract 5.47

I'm calling South Africa, which is an amazing country, while in UK the people are quite rude. (*Roberto, current agent*)

Alex told me that what in Italy is polite is considered rude in the UK.

Extract 5.48

There's someone (…) very strong like Italian accent, (…) [the way he talks to people in Italy] he says in Italy it's perfect, like it's how they do things, but in England definitely not and it is rude ((laughs)), it's very rude. (*Alex, current agent*)

The alterations at issue here concern what outsiders might think of as small variations, such as accents, integrating politeness formulas, or adding one's location to the script. Some of these strategies may have been listed on the country-specific objection-handling sheets given to agents during training. They are not only meant to be rebuttal strategies, but to help agents use the script as a shield to protect themselves from potential rudeness and insults on the phone and if possible avoid them. The idea is that if one uses many politeness formulas, the other person is also more inclined to be polite to them.

In addition to the tips listed on the objection handing sheets, callers try to take advantage of their knowledge and first-hand experience of ideological representations and stereotypes in their countries of specific groups or accents. The extract below suggests that Roberto also plays with stereotypes, such as the capacity of a strong Italian (Napolitanean) accent to evoke connotations of the Mafia among the British.

Extract 5.49

The guy with the Italian accent, Roberto, half the time I don't understand a thing he says, but he talks to the managers for ages. They are interested in talking to him just because he is so funny [David imitates his accent and repeats what Roberto always says on the phone] (…) "My name is Provezano" (…) it just sounds like the mafia films, Provezano (…). I had a discussion with him today, I was like: "why do you always say Provezano?" [Roberto uses only his surname on the phone instead of introducing himself by his Christian name Roberto]. He was like "I don't like Roberto. It's too common." [David imitates Roberto's Naples accent with his very high-pitched voice]. He was like "if I say Roberto it's like he is my friend or something" [again imitating the accent]. (…) I was like "fair enough." (*David, current agent*)

Other agents reported that manipulating gender and sexuality might work to a caller's advantage if handled carefully.

Extract 5.50

If you call as a woman to men, men will listen to women. It's just that gender thing. I don't care, you know, what country you're from, it's the same. It's the same in Finland and it's the same in the UK. (*Siiri, substitute team leader*) (Source: Woydack and Rampton 2016)

Extract 5.51

I think gender makes a difference. I think it's easier for girls (…) because (…) I think maybe 90 percent of the IT managers are men. (*Sonia, current agent*)

Extract 5.52

One flirts with men. Flirting makes life a lot easier. If you realize that it might work, then by all means use that strategy. (*Vanessa, current agent*)

In the cases described here, agents use the act of laughing as a strategy in the same way they use the politeness tokens built into the scripts. It helps them protect themselves from possible insults and sets up a friendly mood.

Field Note Entry 5.2 Laughing and flirting on the phone

It was a tradition among female team leaders to advise female agents whenever talking to men to "laugh on the phone," whenever they are not sure what to say, the situation is awkward, and/or to break the ice. That day there was a new cohort of female German speaking callers from Austria, Switzerland, and southern Germany. Ada had trained and instructed them to laugh and flirt with men on the phone as much as they could. The next day, I overheard how they did exactly that. Most of them were laughing hard on the phone. There was in particular one agent who told me she was a "Swabian Bavarian" [Swabia is a region in Southern Germany. It borders with Bavaria. Usually one is either Swabian or Bavarian, not both] who had a bit of a funny and exotic accent in German [I had never heard it before and it made me chuckle a bit] combined with a friendly high-pitched voice. But she used it to her full advantage. I could tell that men really enjoyed talking to her and even started a personal conversation with her. One person even asked her out. At times, however, considering the high dial rates it can be problematic for female callers to have personal conversations and then have to end them because of the time constraints they face, even though the other person on the phone seems to enjoy themselves.

Data logging

Agents calls entail data entry and logging which affects the life of a script. The data reported by agents is reviewed by campaign managers and team leaders who them summarize the reports for upstairs management and clients. When the reported data is unsatisfactory in terms of campaign results, clients and upstairs management may suggest a rewrite of the script or more likely end the campaign and thereby, end the life of the script. Agents themselves may also modify their hand-annotated script if their results as recorded through data entry are poor.

In the remainder of the chapter, I use the terms data entry, logging, and updating the database to refer to the same process. Strictly speaking, logging refers to the selection of given options by clicking on them with the mouse, whereas data entry describes the process of typing new information into the database. Although the importance of these activities varies with the types of campaign, any phone call should lead to some form of information logging.

Updating the database is not only in the interest of upstairs, but also of campaign managers, team leaders, and agents. Good data can improve call outcomes and more importantly, lead generation. For high-end campaigns, agents need to obtain answers to specific questions over the phone. The more questions and the more information obtained over the phone, often through skilled transposition by agents, the more clients will be charged. This information is very valuable to them and only obtainable over the phone. Agents will summarize the answers to the questions as part of the data entry. These will be shared with the client or sold to the client at an additional cost. If agents fail to log their data accurately, the value of the company's records and its productivity are compromised. When agents make errors, the company risks poor practices in-house with upstairs and poor relations with clients. If the contact is logged as a lead but the agent did not speak to the contact or did not obtain their consent for a callback, this is breaking the law, and clients might cancel the campaign and never do business again with CallCentral. The heart of client interactions with CallCentral is in the data logging processes.

Agents record information in the call center's database from every call they make. Some of this is available to clients in the form of statistics. Clients evaluate CallCentral and the success of their campaign on the basis of such data and can always ask for a new script or even cancel the campaign. This puts pressure on CallCentral to communicate via their data reliably with their clients and CallCentral management transmits this pressure to agents. However, both agents and the company at large benefit from good data management.

The reliability of the database, which consists of valid contacts at various businesses around the world, drives company assessments and operations and is therefore crucial to productivity. Much time is devoted to training new agents in database entering practices. It is cost-efficient for the company to have agents keep the database clean and up-to-date rather than buying expensive new lists of contacts from other companies (see also Woydack and Rampton 2016).

The same database is used at all sites and divisions of CallCentral worldwide. The more reliable the database, the more valuable it is. Accidentally deleting information or mis-entering data affects campaigns at all company sites including those in the United States, Australia, and other European and Asian countries. Thus, agents feel pressure to handle data entry effectively.

Indeed, the database is one of the call center's prime assets. The main database with its data lists has been populated over years with increasingly accurate and detailed information. Agents can recite the script directly to the contact person and make leads instead of cleaning and populating the database. Clients know that this means agents can pitch their script and their message directly to many hundreds of businesses a day, and agents can ask the contacts in the database for the information the client desires. This is emphasized in the initial sales meeting with a client. As Jenny explains,

Extract 5.53

So (…) a client will come to us, and at that point a sales person will meet up with them, have a conversation, and tell them what our database can do for them and pitch for them. (*Jenny, senior campaign manager*)

I describe below the five different types of data entry so far encountered in this book, and demonstrate how these influence the adaptation of the script by agents.

1) **Logging call outcomes:**

After every call, agents fill out a field for "call outcomes." A call outcome has to be generated by the agent with every call. Although the range of the outcomes vary from campaign to campaign, there are some standard possibilities, such as: *no answer, voicemail, call back, bad data (such as private phone numbers or invalid contact numbers), and lead.* This information allows clients to assess the success of a campaign. When leads are fewer than expected, a script may be recalled and rewritten, or the campaign is cancelled altogether. If it is a problem only for a specific agent, they themselves may modify their script or be advised by team leaders on how to improve it.

2) Updating the individual company record information:

Ideally, in line with the brief, agents should always update the following fields after every call:

- Name of the company called
- Company's address
- Phone number
- Fax number
- Corporate website
- Industry
- Employee size
- Updated contact name and details:

  – job title(s) (in English)
  – job function
  – email address
  – telephone extension
  – If the contact has left, it is crucial to log this.

- If any of the other contacts listed for the company have left or if names have been misentered previously, these errors should be logged.
- Any new contacts and their job titles obtained over the phone need to be added

It usually takes several minutes to update, enter, and save everything. If the database is populated by poor information or is incomplete, it is more difficult for agents to reach the appropriate IT personnel and thus their success rate in obtaining leads will be lower. As mentioned above, when the number of leads being obtained is inadequate, scripts may be modified either upstairs with clients or by individual agents hoping to improve their performances. Such adjustments and repairs to scripts are in vain if the database remains inadequately developed.

3) Filling out the fields for different types of campaigns

Whenever a contact answers all the questions on the script (producing a "lead"), callers need to enter the responses in the database. There are several section headings on the computer screen that correspond to the questions on the master script to help them with this.

For the anonymized BIS model campaign, there would be three questions.

(a) Is the individual responsible for IT security within their organization?
(b) Agreed to receive the report?
(c) Agreed to be contacted by BIS (the client)?

In general, BANT and nurturing campaigns' master scripts have more (profiling) questions. So agents fill out more fields on the screen than for engagement campaigns. Data entry is done after the call. There is a rule that everything is first written down by hand and then typed into the computer after the completion of the call. This avoids the potential loss of information from multitasking while the conversation is going on, and offers a safety net in case of a computer crash during a call.

The quality of information received from IT personnel contacted is assessed regularly by managers and clients. When the feedback is poor, again, scripts may be held responsible and manipulated.

4) Writing call-specific summary remarks

Agents should save a summary of what has happened when they tried to call a company from their calling list. As campaigns often run several weeks, these remarks may range from abbreviations like VM (for *voicemail*) or N/A (no *no answer*), to long comments spanning several paragraphs. These comments are not saved permanently, just for the duration of the campaign.

Such notes can help a campaign manager and team leader: (i) understand any problems with the campaign, (ii) recognize when agents are phoning the same company needlessly, or (iii) assist a caller in remembering what happened or to whom they talked. These data fields, too, can lead to adjustments to a script if management finds consistent problems occurring.

5) Lead remarks for BANT and nurturing campaigns

For high-end campaigns, callers summarize their phone conversations for every lead, generating "lead remarks." These documents, typically about two pages and written in English, are forwarded to the client. From the campaign managers' point of view, good lead remarks contain specific information that could only have been obtained through a phone conversation with the contact (for example, the nature of problems they have had with a particular software brand).

These remarks represent another criterion that allows a client to assess the quality of the work. For this reason, the remarks must be thoughtfully composed. Callers are expected by the downstairs management to personalize their script sufficiently and use the consultative approach in such a way as to engage the contact and obtain the desired information. There is an internal quality control process in place to ensure that several team leaders have read the lead remarks before they are sent to the client. If the results reported from the statistics such as the dial reports or the lead remarks are considered poor, most likely the campaign manager will make hand-written changes to the master script and share these with agents.

The data entry process is time-intensive, but many callers mention the importance of a good database for carrying out their job. For instance, Juan notes:

Extract 5.54

> I think the key [for this job] is the database. If you have very accurate information you can get very good service and you come straight to the people you need. (*Juan, current agent*)

David considers updating the database so important that he would like to lower the call rate. Since entering data often requires more time than the calls themselves, David argues that it would be useful to devote the time needed to the entries without feeling pressured to be constantly on the phone:

Extract 5.55

If I was in charge personally, I would lower the calls, the amount of calls you need to make per day (…). The main reason why I would do that is for people to put better information into the systems [database]. I think that's 50 percent of the job. (*David, current agent*)

Nevertheless, many are aware that partly because of pressure to meet targets and the lack of training, many (newer) agents do not update the database. As David observes:

Extract 5.56

The way it currently works is that people are under pressure to make calls so they will write something in the remarks [personal agent remarks - data type entry 4] or write something up quickly, but they aren't gonna go into the whole system [database] and save it, because you have to go back saving it three or four times. People can't bother. They don't have time. (…). So (…) the system [the database] kind of goes a bit out of sync. It will be like 5 names and you don't know who is who and it just makes your job like 5 times harder. (…) They just take it away from the team. (…) It's like they really don't understand but people who have been here long enough understand that this will come back round to you at some point (…) (*David, current agent*)

However, Yasmin, who recently joined the call center, told me that it was only after the special database training session upstairs (see Field note entry 5.3) that she understood the need for updating.

Extract 5.57

After the first training if it's not a lead I don't spend time updating. (…) [Only after] the special training (…) I (…) realized that updating (…) [is] so important. (*Yasmin, new agent*)

Field Note Entry 5.3 The special database training for new agents

After continuous complaints from the team leaders and upstairs about agents' failure to do correct data logging, Jenny had enough and booked a meeting room upstairs. She took all the team leaders and the newer agents to the 'Florence' meeting room upstairs. [In all my time there, I had never seen agents being taken upstairs, apart from when downstairs was operating beyond capacity]. I can still remember the people working upstairs, how their jaws dropped open when they saw twenty agents following Jenny to 'Florence'. They were simply staring at them in disbelief. It was my impression that Jenny wanted the new callers to see upstairs to understand what a great company they worked for so they could identify with it. It was said downstairs that agents, all of whom are employed temporarily, had little incentive to update the database, in particular if they only stayed at the call center for two weeks anyway. During our stay in "Florence," Jenny spent a lot of time explaining the function of each section on the database.

Later in the afternoon, I overheard Jenny saying that the operations manager was not happy about the long training session upstairs, as too much time had been lost off the phone. According to the operations manager, every minute agents spend off the phone (including training), the company loses revenue. Apparently, people upstairs had also complained about agents coming upstairs. (Adapted from Woydack and Rampton 2016)

Similarly, Stuart believes that often agents do not understand why the database requires updating:

Extract 5.58

I think we baffle callers as to why we make the demands that we make [about data entry], so maybe if we explain that, '…well because we need this for this data section and this for this data section.' I think that would be a way to improve training. (*Stuart, team leader*)

Experienced agents like Miguel suggest that there should be more training on this.

Extract 5.59

Training about how to keep the database clean (…), to me that's really important (…). It's really a slow job to keep the database as clean and as neat as possible, but I'm sure that it pays back, because maybe you are not saving time for yourself but I'm sure that you're saving time for the next guy who's calling your contact. (…) You should take your time to (…) to keep it clean (…). When you find out that someone's not working there any more, to put that (…) instead of thinking that you're wasting time and you need to make the other call. But (…) if you ask for someone who's not working there anymore, then you have their immediate objection [and you need objection handling]. (*Miguel, current agent*)

Miguel pointed out that if agents operate on the wrong information, they are less likely to be able to pitch the script, or will have less time to do so. This affects their transposition as they need to hit the dial rate of 200–250 calls a day. Moreover, if callers do not enter data correctly, the statistics do not reveal that the data is a problem. Consequently, upstairs and the client may wrongly assume that the master script is the issue and will provide agents with a new one rather than pressuring the agents to log better data. Management may even purchase contact lists at this point—an expensive and often inefficient alternative to agent-centered data entry. The failure to update the database and perform correct logging has implications for callers' performance and the script's career.

Having a poor database creates even more tension for agents, in addition to the pressures to log their data consistently and reliably, to personalize the master script and consult with interlocutors, and to make dial rates. Even so, agents come to recognize the value of the database and continue to lobby for lower dial rate targets to allow them to proceed with their tasks adequately.

We have seen a variety of ways in which database entry may influence the career of the script and its transposition. These are

(i) Agents may choose not to update the database so they can spend more time on the phone and follow the master script properly. But the lack of updating may lead to an end to the scripts' career, as the data for calling will continuously get worse. This will then make it difficult and more time-consuming for callers to get through to people and pitch the script. Second, without correct data logging there are no reliable statistics or feedback produced for upstairs (and the client). They may not know what is going on, and may incorrectly believe that the script needs to be replaced by a new one in order to resolve the issue.

(ii) Updating the database is slow; it causes agents to lose time they need to spend on the phone to meet their high dial rates. Because of time constraints, callers are not always able to ask all the questions from the master script and therefore obtain less valuable information for their lead remarks. Subsequently, the client may complain about the lack of quality (evident from the lead remarks) and as a result ask for a new script or cancel the campaign.

(iii) The content of information logged in several of the entry practices allows agents to reflect on their relative success in a particular campaign. When call outcomes are weak, an agent may modify a script to better consult with interlocutors or to present a more personable and comfortable approach to contacts. In addition, when results are poor, management or clients may revise scripts or cancel the campaign.

Conclusion: agency in calling—beyond the dualism of control and resistance

The master script undergoes various transformations. Figure 5.1 summarizes this third major stage in the trajectory of the master script—its enactment and use by agents. Most agents use entextualization and retextualization processes throughout a campaign. To maximize their success in generating leads for a client, they make a wide range of phonological, lexico-grammatical, pragmatic, and sociolinguistic adjustments in line with a plurality of influences on and off the phone. The idea is to own the script so that their delivery is natural and engaging. Agents are encouraged

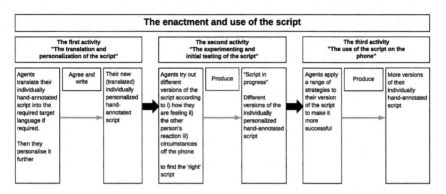

Fig. 5.1 The enactment and use of the script

to personalize their scripts by adjusting text while preserving the skeletal structure. They are encouraged to use a consultative approach, and to adopt other strategies to meet their targets and obtain specific information (see also Woydack and Rampton 2016). However, the contradicting expectations of upstairs for verbatim delivery of scripts means that callers' transformations to the script are monitored as much as possible to be sure they maintain the gist and structure of a script. Data entry and statistics compilations typically cue campaign managers that something is off in an agent's delivery. Otherwise they are left to make the best adjustments they can.

Despite agents' many modifications to a script, they claim that the essential content and message of the script remains intact. Whether or not this is the case is a complex matter and even the corporation's own sophisticated monitoring system struggles with making the distinction. Nonetheless, at the callers' level there is more emphasis on producing a record after every call (lead remarks and data entry) than on conveying a message verbatim from the client. Callers believe the record constitutes the end product for the client. Accordingly, the script obtains a different significance and function from those observed at the team leaders' level and upstairs. Callers now talk of the script as a tool they need to refashion so they can enter data and deliver the product the client desires. For callers, the script has become more of a means to an end and less a definitive document in itself. Consequently, callers (and team leaders) talk of standardization as an abstract ideal not bound to the verbatim spoken performance of the script, but linked to the standardization of the meaning of the script's essential content and a typed record on the organization's database.

This means the call center operations are governed by an implicit contradiction that seldom surfaces and that works to the advantage of the firm. The master script is a product that the company sells to the client. It is conceived of as a concrete fixed entity on the basis of which agents' performances can be measured and assessed so that any given campaign is monitored to allow for adjustments from upstairs along the way. Downstairs, however, the script is a tool that is collectively and/or sequentially altered by the call center managers, team leaders, and agents who refashion it in pursuit of goals: leads, lead remarks, populating and updating the database, and disseminating the key points the call center is paid to deliver.

So where does the description of the script's enactment and use leave us?

As mentioned previously, sociologists and sociolinguists writing from a neo- Foucauldian or neo-Marxist perspective tend to take a critical view of standardization, the practice of scripting, and the related surveillance that is part of it. Key to this discussion has been assessing how a combination of scripting and surveillance affects workers and their well-being. For instance, Cameron argues that the stronger the "control over worker's performance" the more limited agents' "own autonomy" (2000, 98) and that "much of the work that people do in most call centers *could* in principle be done by a machine" (Cameron 2000, 94).

Equally, Belt and colleagues argue that by definition, scripting and "the nature of work organization used in call centers acts to *constrain* skill development" (Belt, Richardson, and Webster 2002, 28; see also Korczynski 2002, 43; Ritzer 1998, 64). Accordingly, agents are expected to be discontented with standardization and if not, according to the literature, they are dupes of the system. Those who are discontented are expected to resist the standardization practices oppressing them; the non-discontented are ignored. In fact many researchers, those using both the neo-Foucauldian and neo-Marxist approaches, assess the impact and success of the control measures by analyzing the resistance of workers (McPhail 2002, 44). Fernie and Metcalf (1998) argue, however, that the panoptic control or prison-like environment achieved through technological advances denies any space for collectively expressed resistance and very little, if any, for the individual.

Industrial sociologists traditionally have preferred to focus on open resistance spurred by workers' loss of agency rather than focusing on how workers might adjust themselves to an oppressive environment, reclaiming their agency. Survey and questionnaires have been the dominant research tools rather than ethnography. As a result, less attention has been paid to more subtle forms of resistance among workers, for example when agents beat the system by hanging up on customers or by taking sick leave. The literature has not examined non-compliance with scripting procedure at all. Perhaps one could argue that studies that focus on instances of resistance are focusing on agency. However, as Mumby (2005, 27–28) has pointed out, much of the previous research on resistance fails "to adequately theorize the possibilities for human agency at the level of everyday organizing" (2005, 27–28) and remains caught within a duality of control and resistance, rarely going beyond these poles. Mumby (2005) concludes that although employee resistance features to some degree "in both forms of analysis [Foucauldian and Marxian], it is usually read as subsumed within, and reproductive of, these control mechanisms" (2005, 26). In addition, all the resistance addressed in the studies is individual, often even guerrilla-like, but never collective.

An exception to the previous research on standardization, resistance, and agency is Leidner (1993, 5) who instead suggests "rather than assuming that workers who do not resist routines are either miserable or duped, it would seem more fruitful to consider whether there are circumstances in which routines, even imposed routines, can be useful to workers." Leidner is one researcher who explicitly points out the advantages of standardization and scripting. She bases her more positive evaluation of standardization on her ethnographic study of McDonalds, in which neither staff at McDonalds nor service recipients oppose the use of scripts or their controlling nature. Cook-Gumperz (2001,123) summarizes some of the reasons why the staff in Leidner's study supported scripts:

With possession of a script most situational risks are neutralized or made safe, so allowing workers to do their job by merely keeping to the script itself. The result is that the built-in politeness tokens create a completely routinized interactional environment where the exchange design assures both equal treatment for the customer and also provides for the customers managed compliance in cooperating with the worker. Workers find that politeness eases their own vulnerability to personal exposure. Thus, politeness routines solve a structural problem of service encounters by creating an interactional "safe zone" in which worker and customer come together in a clearly defined situation with a goal (Cook-Gumperz 1991 cited in Cook-Gumperz 2001). It is this which explains their readiness to adhere to the script although it only permits minimal personalized variations. (Cook-Gumperz 2001, 123)

Yet it is important to point out a vital difference between the script of the McDonald franchise that Leidner studied and my field site. That is, the script her informants were given did not have to be translated (under most circumstances) and was designed with an audience of second or third or subsequent generations of Americans in mind. On the other hand, the call center job at CallCentral, by definition, involves dealing with multiple countries and languages. The master script is originally written in English for a British audience, but after agents' training, they are asked to translate it into other target languages and adapt it accordingly. This adaptation includes the politeness tokens and other pragmatic features relevant to the local contexts (e.g., Extracts 5.2, 5.48, 5.49). However, as noted in this chapter, the translation process is often chaotic (see Field note entry 5.1: Translating master scripts), leading agents to complain that they need to re-translate a script (e.g., Extract 5.8) before they can personalize it even though it had already been translated beforehand by other agents.

From the discussion so far we have seen that agents support scripting as a tool that helps them carry out their job well. Despite their clear advocacy for scripting and the desire to do their job well, at first sight the changes they introduce into their call scripts appear to be at odds with Cook-Gumperz's explanation that service sector workers support scripts because of politeness tokens and the protection these entail. That is, it would appear that if agents personalize a script, which is said to involve "selling yourself" (David Extract 5.34), flirting with men on the phone (e.g., Extract 5.52), and revealing personal things about oneself, their script may risk losing its neutral feel and its built-in politeness tokens to other approaches. A caller may become more vulnerable to personal insults from the person on the phone if personalization goes too far.

We have seen from the description of the script's last career stage that agents are aware of the differences in cross-cultural politeness and realize that getting politeness tokens right eases their own vulnerability to personal exposure. The fact that several of my informants discuss and generalize "rudeness" cross-culturally, based on their calling experience, suggests that they have experienced it first-hand (e.g., Extracts 5.46 and 5.47). So personalizing scripts and re-writing them can be in an agent's own interest. They can create a calling procedure that encourages friendly and hopefully successful interactions. To the extent that personalization and listening or consulting are successful, the client and upstairs management also benefit.

Literature on standardization practices, scripting, and monitoring might lead one to argue that the agents' recontextualizations of a script represent acts of resistance against the script and the management. However, this misses the observation that their transpositions are intended to benefit the client and upstairs management. Based on the observations and data I have presented, I argue that "resistance" is too simplistic a word for what occurs in agents' calling and transpositioning practices. There are at least three reasons why agents' changes to their scripts are not acts of resistance.

First, agents believe they are acting in the best interests of the company. They have no reason to be aware of any details of upstairs' contractual agreements with clients, and are encouraged to apply a set of guiding strategies to modify the script. Most agents only stay at the call center for a few weeks. This means skills need to be rapidly acquired and applied, creating a challenging work setting. Their focus is on campaign goals and development of a script that maximizes results. Those who stay on longer, even the more seasoned, still have no interaction with upstairs or the client in part simply because of the physical separation between them. In fact, agents have little contact with the campaign managers, the mid-level supervisors who delegate responsibilities to team leaders for close work with agents. I found that not even team leaders were aware of the contractual agreement given to the client (except for Stuart who had been in lots of meeting with the client and had been working at CallCentral for over four years). In fact, even I was unaware of the verbatim rule until I learned about it by accident two years after I was already a team leader. I read about it on a document given to me by a campaign manager who trusted me.

In the interview extracts, callers express a strong conviction that any of their hand-written or oral alterations to the script are within their allowed framework (the skeletal approach). In essence, they stress that despite their rewording, they still mention the key points (and the eight sections) and do their job properly (e.g., Extract 5.35).

Second, the effort agents make to improve the script is a sign of their job commitment. This is evident in the various strategies they apply to enhance the appeal of their script and in their collaborations with peers to revise the script effectively. They clearly are not just "animators," but have in some sense become "authors" on the phone with partial agency. The script becomes a tool they refashion in the client's, company's, and their own best interests as workers.

It is worth mentioning how many of my informants used the term "own" in reference to the script. Several said, for instance, you "make the script your own." The feeling of owning the script also emerged in Chapter 4, for example, in how leaders look after the paper copy of their own script. Agents, too, treat their modified scripts with respect and preserve them in the spaces provided for their storage. There is thus a bond between script and agent once the work of transposing is set and the calls are in process. Consequently, if a script is perceived as one's own, there is unlikely to be a need to resist it.

Thirdly, while agents are supportive of a script and do not perceive it as a problem, they complain about the inflexible, mandatory, and unrealistic targets which they feel impede their efforts to fully convey a script to interlocutors and may compromise the important data entry phase of their work. This in turn can result in confusion and unnecessary script changes. As a result, agents ask for lower targets so they can communicate all the essential content from a script in their speech on the phone and do

proper data entry as well. Several callers argue that it is in their best interest to do data entry after every call and that only inexperienced and new
agents resist this process. Equally, in the previous chapter it emerged that
when the dial rates were raised to impossible levels, agents responded by
reluctantly cutting important sections of the script in an effort to cope.
Team leaders then stepped in to tell agents what they could and could not
leave out. Even in this case, however, agents' actions were not motivated
by resistance. They took steps to create the least damage possible to the
quality of the script and to the record (cf. Chapter 4 Field note entry 4.3)
even as they modified it to allow them to accede to the competing
demands of management.

References

Belt, Vicki, Ranald Richardson, and Juliet Webster. 2002. Women, Social Skill
    and Interactive Service Work in Telephone Call Centres. *New Technology,
    Work and Employment* 17 (1): 20–34.
Cameron, Deborah. 2000. *Good to Talk?* London: Sage.
Cook-Gumperz, Jenny. 2001. Cooperation, Collaboration and Pleasure in
    Work. Culture in Communication: Analyses of Intercultural Situations. In
    Culture in Communication: Analyses of Intercultural Situations, ed. Aldo Di
    Luzio, Susanne Günthner, and Franca Orletti, 117–139. Amsterdam: John
    Benjamins Publishing.
Fernie, Sue, and David Metcalf. 1998. *(Not) Hanging on the Telephone: Payment
    Systems in the New Sweatshops*. London: London School of Economics,
    Centre for Economic Performance.
Korczynski, Marek. 2002. *Human Resource Management in Service Work*,
    Management, Work and Organisations. Basingstoke: Palgrave Macmillan.
Leidner, Robin. 1993. *Fast Food, Fast Talk: Service Work and the Routinization of
    Everyday Life*. Berkeley: University of California Press.
McPhail, Brenda. 2002. *What Is 'on the Line' in Call Centre Studies? A Review of
    Key Issues on Academic Literature*. University of Toronto. http://www3.fis.
    utoronto.ca/research/iprp/publications/mcphail-cc.pdf
Mumby, Dennis K. 2005. Theorizing Resistance in Organization Studies: A
    Dialectical Approach. *Management Communication Quarterly* 19 (1): 19–44.
Ritzer, George. 1998. *The McDonaldization Thesis: Explorations and Extensions*.
    London / Thousand Oaks: Sage.

Smith, Dorothy E. 1996. The Relations of Ruling: A Feminist Inquiry. *Studies in Cultures, Organizations and Societies* 2 (2): 171–190.

Woydack, Johanna. 2016. Superdiversity and a London Multilingual Call Centre. In *Engaging Superdiversity: Recombining Spaces, Times and Language Practices*, ed. Karel Arnaut, Martha Sif Karrebaek, Massimiliano Spotti, and Jan Blommaert, vol. 7, 220–251. Bristol: Multilingual Matters.

Woydack, Johanna, and Ben Rampton. 2016. Text Trajectories in a Multilingual Call Centre: The Linguistic Ethnography of a Calling Script. *Language in Society* 45 (05): 709–732.

6

Standardization and Agency Intertwined

In this book I set out to develop through ethnography a better understanding of managers' and workers' perceptions and practices entailing scripts and standardization in call centers. This book is the first, to my knowledge, to use long-term ethnography in an outbound call center, and to use the textual trajectory of a script within a call center to do it.

I started by arguing that the sociological and sociolinguistic findings from call center studies, to date, tend to "evoke a negative image of call centers as digital communication factories of the post-industrial service economy" (cf. Shire et al. 2002, 3). For instance, Holman and Fernie (2000, 1) note that the majority of call center studies "conjure up an image of oppressive, stifling working conditions, constant surveillance, poor job satisfaction." Moreover, I have argued that in the literature, call centers are intrinsically linked with standardization, and that the increased use of scripting is seen to represent a significant development in the intensification of Taylorization of white-collar work. This has further contributed to a negative image.

In fact, studies of standardization in workplaces more generally take a negative approach. There are three reasons for this. First, as Timmermans and Epstein (2010) suggest in a review article on standardization in sociology, a long history of social theory dating back to Marx and Weber uses standard-

© The Author(s) 2019

J. Woydack, *Linguistic Ethnography of a Multilingual Call Center:*
London Calling, Communicating in Professions and Organizations,
https://doi.org/10.1007/978-3-319-93323-8_6

ization in a derogatory sense—as a process leading to homogeneity, deskilling, and dehumanization. They believe that this tendency persists today and is evident in Ritzer's McDonaldization (1998). Second, as Leidner (1993, 22) and Mumby (2005, 25) have proposed, because of the researchers' epistemological positioning, most studies overstate the employer's success in imposing standardization routines, supposing that such practices inevitably serve the goals intended by management. The third reason for the negative view stems from the methods researchers have employed in studying call centers. Researchers have found it difficult to gain access, perform participant observation, and conduct interviews with any of the call center staff, so they have relied, in the main, on questionnaires and surveys.

For this reason, many researchers could not observe first-hand how standardization is implemented and how it works on a daily basis. Observing standardization in practice is required not only for obtaining a more balanced view, but also for a complete picture of the situation. Standardization in practice is not always what it seems from the outside, a fact that has been shown repeatedly in ethnographies of factories. Often a vivid "underlife" is exposed on the shop floor with workers and lower managers working their way around the standardized routines designed by upper management (e.g., Burawoy 1979; Linstead 1985; Warde 1992).

So with this book, I convey a more subtle understanding of standardization in call centers that emerges from ethnographic research, allowing me to test the position that standardization is thoroughly oppressive. I suggest that new insights can be achieved through qualitative methods, most importantly long-term ethnography, combined with a dynamic focus on scripts. I summarize here the benefits and rationale for my ethnographic methods and my focus on scripts.

Advantages of ethnographic methods for revealing complexities of corporate hierarchies and subjectivities within them

Ethnography has been defined as "deep immersion into the life of a people. (…) One learns their language and tries to learn the mode of life. One learns by participant observation, by living as well as viewing the new patterns of life" (Keesing 1981, 5–6). My book is not an ethnography in the traditional sense, because I did not focus on a small-scale distant village in a developing country, nor was I an outsider. In fact, having worked alongside agents has made me an insider, which can have benefits, as O'Reilly summarizes:

> Insiders (...) blend in more, gain more rapport, participate more easily, have more linguistic competence with which to ask more subtle questions on more complex issues, and are better at reading non-verbal communications. (...) They get beyond the ideal to the real, daily lived, and backstage experiences. Rather than *describing* the unconscious grammar of the community, their ethnographies are *expressions* of it, the result of a superior insider knowledge gained through primary socialization. (O'Reilly 2009, 114)

So let us see how O'Reilly's quote applies to this book.

As an employee, I had none of the access problems that so many other researchers have had. In fact, the first contribution I am able to make is to provide the first ethnographic study of an outbound call center. The second contribution is that with the benefit of being an insider and having full access, I did not have to rely on questionnaires. Instead, I could observe my participants and their activities and then ask informed "and more subtle" (O'Reilly 2009, 114) questions during the interviews, because of "my superior insider knowledge gained through primary socialization" (O'Reilly 2009, 114).

Thirdly, I offer insights into types of participants who have been marginalized and overlooked in previous non-ethnographic studies. These new insights emerged through the mapping of a script's textual trajectories that encompass the entire organization, and through field notes on the surrounding "real life back-stage" activities during the script's career (O'Reilly 2009, 114). Chapters 2, 3, 4, and 5 have shown that campaign managers and team leaders are important figures whose interpretations and actions influence proceedings on the floor downstairs. With the exception of Houlihan's unpublished PhD thesis (2003) written from a human resource perspective, no research has addressed how the middle management or team leaders in call centers perceive standardization or work with it on a daily basis. Discussions of team leaders or middle managers in previous call center research has been limited to presenting them as "supervisors" who are part of a system, but not as a significant interest group with the capacity to act differently from their superordinate line managers upstairs.

Benefits of focusing on the script as the main object of analysis

Drawing on my ethnographic field notes and interviews with agents, in Chapter 2 I described the field site from the point a view of a new agent and with interview extracts. It emerged that for the management upstairs and downstairs, the script is an important means to achieve predictability, calculability, efficiency, and control on the one hand, and maintain flexibility on the other. We further saw how scripts underpin many aspects of the call center's organization and are an agreed-upon reference point for (i) communication between agents and people on the phone, (ii) training of new and current agents, (iii) qualitative and quantitative measurement (generation of statistics) of the agents' and scripts' successes, (iv) hiring practices, and (v) agents' pay and bonus structures. In view of this discovery, in Chapters 3, 4, and 5 I pursued the career of a script from its production to its use on the phone in more detail.

But following the script's trajectories has other advantages. First, the academic literature often regards the script as the symbol of "standardization" *per se* in the service sector. Second, in the case of my field site, all participants are involved with it at some point. Third, this cross-hierarchical involvement allowed me to explore perceptions of scripts held by managers, team leaders, and agents, as well as their handlings of scripts.

Advantages of tracking textual trajectories over time, space, and personnel

My ethnography is designed to investigate the accuracy of previous research on call center management. They have seen scripts as inflexible standardized documents created at the top of company hierarchies with expectations that they will remain unchanged through the various subsequent work phases. Researchers taking this stance overstate employers' successes in imposing scripts on their workers. They presume that the practices of callers inevitably fulfill goals established by management in their contracts with clients in precisely specified ways.

In contrast, a trajectory approach like the one adopted here reveals the conceptualization of scripts from diverse perspectives in an organization. The perspectives come from primary management upstairs and campaign managers, team leaders, and callers on the floor downstairs. When compared with questionnaire and interview methods dominating earlier research, my focus on text trajectories draws attention to staff often marginalized or overlooked by non-ethnographic studies. The account presented in this book has provided a prominent place for primary management upstairs, mid-level call center managers and team leaders, and call center agents at the end of the chain. I demonstrate through careful analysis of practice that conceptions of scripts vary according to one's corporate position. Rather than "supervisors" sandwiched into an intermediate position in a top-down system (S. Taylor 1998, 95; Fernie and Metcalf 1998; Cameron 2000, 117), team leaders and middle managers alter courses of action and redesign textual documents created by upstairs managers and clients. Agents may diverge even further. In fact, the description of the script trajectory analyzed here shows that in real time, all participants—agents, team leaders, call center managers, and upstairs management —display agency and the capacity to "to act otherwise" in either entextualizing a script initially or retextualizing it in practice (see also Woydack and Rampton 2016).

We have seen that transformations of an original script in the language in which it is first written is a reflective process that can emerge orally or in hand-written annotations. Translation is another phase of script implementation that almost inevitably leads to transpositions. And data entry that results from the use of scripts has an impact on script documents indirectly. These significant forms of agency may have been overlooked in studies that draw only on interviews or questionnaires. Such methods are typically based on researchers' preconceived hypotheses and fail to take into account activities that emerge in practice as ideal scripts composed in securing a client are implemented by calling agents with the guidance of their campaign managers and team leaders. These practices take shape in work that scholars who are outside the industry may have mistaken for marginal back-stage activities. Notions of what constitutes a script and how it should be used depend on the hierarchical position of the participant. This only becomes evident from following the script through its full trajectory. Indeed, the "back-stage" activities (O'Reilly 2009, 114) I observed call into question the notion that call center work is oppressive and unskilled, a notion prominent in previous research. Instead I suggest that mid-level management and callers have agentive orientations and practices in the service of company goals.

Traditionally, analysis in previous call center studies has proposed that deviations from calling scripts are indicators of agents' resistance or are self-consciously "disruptive behavior" (Ackroyd and Thompson 1999; Cameron 2000; Bain and Taylor 2000). I challenge this view here. I offer instead a nuanced analysis of textual transpositions that occur in the process of developing call scripts. The transpositions constitute productive agency on behalf of the goals of the company. These transpositions occur both in advance of calling (when the script is translated or modified to suit a caller's style) and in the midst of call interactions (as agents adjust to their interlocutors).

Agents adopt scripts within the framework they are taught with the goal of generating qualitative leads that they believe the client desires. They are unaware of the client's and upstairs management's view of scripts as documents to be implemented verbatim. In line with what the team leaders have told them, agents understand standardization as the process of adapting a skeletal structure and its significant functional goals to a conversation. Acutely conscious of the need to obtain good leads and data over the phone, agents describe in detail how they adapt their scripts in order to personalize them and modify them in order to meet the unique customs and expectations of those who will be call recipients in places other than London. Thus, the transpositions indicate that from the perspective of agents and team leaders, the script is not static or inflexible, as has been argued in the literature. Chapters 4 and 5 outline the sheer variety of strategies managers, leaders, and agents apply to change a script. I describe the steps involved in re-writing during training sessions, debriefings, or on the phone as agents work in search of the "perfect script" (Extract 5.20).

The call center campaign managers and team leaders believe it is in the client's and company's best interests for agents to obtain reliable, unique information that can only be gained through diplomatic interactions over the phone. They may even recognize that the client and upstairs management push for verbatim readings to fulfill an accountability chain that includes shareholders who ultimately require "objective" evidence of how agents work. This is one way to measure productivity and assure clients that their best interests are driving a campaign. But it may not be the best way to approach another person on the phone. Being aware of an agents' desire to be flexible with a script and notwithstanding the need for monitoring them to assure best practices during calls, downstairs managers allow some leeway concerning the wording of a script as long as the referential topic is standardized and a caller adheres to the eight-section approach. With the script imagined as a scaffold or skeleton, agents can (a) personalize it, and (b) be consultative within an agreed frame.

The trajectory approach has further brought to the surface the need to recognize a qualified place for electronic monitoring in call centers (also compare cf. Lankshear et al. 2001). Because other researchers assumed monitoring produced fidelity in script implementation, the previous literature on call centers has not addressed how scripts are changed as they are translated, annotated, or adapted on the phone. In particular, handwritten changes to a script are easy to miss without the trajectory approach.

Ethnography and the trajectory approach with a view toward transpositions, taken altogether, suggest that the script and accordingly standardization are conceptualized distinctively by the different levels of the call center hierarchy.

Perspectival variation in hierarchies

The different qualitative methods used in Chapters 3, 4, and 5 have shown that the script is conceptualized distinctively upstairs and downstairs. Only upstairs and the client believe no changes will be made to the script and imagine it to be static and to rigidly regulate activities downstairs. In Chapters 4 and 5 I demonstrate that participants further down the hierarchy, at some remove from upstairs, conceptualize the master script as part of a "textual trajectory" during which the script is transformed, often repeatedly. Against this background of perspectival variation, the notion of what *standardized, standard,* or *standardization* means becomes open to variation and interpretation as well.

If understanding the notion of standardization depends on the hierarchical position of the participant, whose understanding does one take? Because of this conundrum I argued that (i) it is important to look at participants' views of the script across all levels of the organization and in diverse activities so the full range of perspectives can be captured, and (ii) it is vital to explore standardization as polysemic by looking at themes traditionally used for understanding standardization in organizations such as resistance, agency, and deskilling. In the sections that follow I summarize the dimensions of variation along which standardization is understood and implemented. I use separate headings to draw out features of the discussions from Chapters 3, 4, and 5. Ultimately many of the themes are interrelated in call center practices. The first theme of note is the existence of "rules within rules" within CallCentral.

Rules within rules

Given the important roles mid-level call center managers and team leaders play in the trajectory of a script, ethnographic insights allow me to offer an understanding of the dynamics that characterize the relationship between upstairs and downstairs. First, efforts on the part of downstairs managers, leaders, and agents are in every instance about cooperation, not resistance. Campaign managers know that not only does a client want to see certain outcomes, but ultimately upstairs has to present a certain product and image in order to sell a campaign, and for there to be further employment for agents. This arrangement includes what Houlihan describes as "rules within rules" (Houlihan 2003, 277). Downstairs must manage the stipulations of the contract with a client and implement the script, sometimes transcending the explicit expectations of company managers. The secrecy around script changes downstairs is part of this. For instance, when the new campaign manager, Eva, accidentally revealed agents' modification practices to an operations manager from upstairs, she was neither aware that these practices must not be mentioned to him nor that they could bring on trouble downstairs. She had yet to learn the segregated rules within the larger framework.

Script changes derived from transformative practices are not deemed "disruptive behavior" downstairs. There they are essential and productive. They are only perceived as disruptive when upstairs managers are explicitly told about them and take exception to them. Another "rule within rules" stipulates that all changes to the script made by agents are handwritten and spoken as these index something unofficial and invisible to upstairs. Agents are not allowed to retype and reprint scripts.

Agents are typically unaware of upstairs' and clients' position on textual fidelity, and any contractual agreement with clients. They are trained to retextualize scripts within a set of well-established procedures and guidelines that maximize opportunities to meet company goals. Individuals downstairs may disagree with the likelihood of success in a campaign given the characteristics of a script when it arrives from upstairs management for implementation. However, rather than an oppositional structure of management control and (individual) worker resistance generating discontent and rebellious strategies, deviation from the original texts occurs collectively downstairs in a well-established, recognized, and efficiently guided, not individualistic process of recrafting (see also Woydack and Rampton 2016).

Closely related to the issue of "rules within rules" described in this section is that of resistance vs. compliance. This question emerges: of the different parties in the call center, who is compliant or resistant or both? Before seeing how the concepts apply to my case study, I take a step back to show how the concept of resistance has been used previously in the literature on call centers and other workplaces.

Creative compliance versus resistance

Resistance has been a major theme in the literature as it is believed that agents must read from a pre-written script (scripted Taylorism) and that this is enforced with strict high tech monitoring that records agents' calls and every click they make on their computers (similar to Foucault's panopticon) (cf. Bain and Taylor 2000). The literature on organizational resistance generally tends to discuss resistance as part of a dualism with control. The majority of call center studies take this approach, that call centers are emblematic panopticons. They hunt for instances involving individual cases of an agent's resistance against scripts. These individuals are framed and celebrated as heroically resisting the computer system that is always watching.

Probably the most famous analysis of resistance in organizations is Burawoy's (1979) neo-Marxist study of a factory in Chicago. As Mumby (2005) argues, Burawoy's approach also suffers from the aforementioned dualism. Burawoy (1979) argues that the conflicts on the shop floor represent a struggle and political game between shop managers and higher management. In the factory where he conducted research, machine operators took regular shortcuts in the game of "making out" (1979, 60). In a regular cycle, their subversions were discovered and higher management, concerned with profit margins, reinforced its authority by imposing new limits on costs and quality. These new rules turned out to be incompatible with the shop floor labor process and had to be relaxed again by the management downstairs. So the struggle persisted. In the end, Burawoy's analysis focuses on how "the game of making out," symbolizing workers' individual attempts to resist (against machines), ends with them "manufacturing their own consent" to the hegemonic management policies (cf. Mumby 2005, 26–27).

Unlike Burawoy (1979), Roy (1959) does not consider game playing in a factory as resistance to managerial control. Instead, he views these practices as practical solutions to coping with a monotonous 12-hour work day. In fact Marchington argues that most workers avoid conflict behavior (1992, 157). In this sense, Roy's game playing could be conceptualized as what Marchington calls "getting by" strategies, not "disruptive actions." With these strategies, workers draw on competencies and tacit skills to mediate their work. Moreover, since the majority of employees take pride in their work and want to meet a certain standard of professionalism, Marchington suggests that they use not only no-conflict "getting by" but also "getting on" strategies. He conceptualizes "getting on" as "pragmatic instrumentalism" (1992, 157)—workers want to contribute with their competencies to the organization's success rather than sabotage it (also cf. Houlihan 2003, 18–20).

Goffman suggests an alternative theorization of "disruptive practices," also considering them an "essential constituent of the self" (1961, 279). In *Asylums*, he looks at the underlife of "total institutions" and provides a framework for uncovering the dialectic between self-definition and the "official self" (1961, 170). He distinguishes between (a) the implicit contract of the organizational relationship that includes incentives (negative sanctions) to perform well, and (b) behaviors considered of value to both the individual and the institution, those of "joint value" that facilitate a "discipline of being" (Houlihan 2003, 23). Goffman contends that in so far as the member of the organization consents to this, he or she has made a primary adjustment, "tacitly accepting a view of what will motivate him, and hence a view of his identity" (1961, 165). Having an official identity along with a self-identity enables the individual to create boundaries and participate in deviant behavior to bypass some of the "organization's assumptions of what he should do and hence what he should be" (Goffman 1961, 172). Goffman calls this "secondary adjustment" (1961, 172). He distinguishes between "disruptive secondary adjustment" (when the "intentions of participants are to abandon the organization or radically alter its structure") and "contained secondary adjustment" (an individual is part of the status quo and non-disruptive, but can mentally tune out the organization) (1961, 180–181). The second type is semi-authorized and tolerated, thus the individual is a participant in the primary contract between member and organization (cf. Houlihan 2003, 22–23).

At first sight, the data presented in Chapters 3, 4, and 5 might suggest Burawoy (1979) is right, that struggles and political games between the shop floor management and upstairs and the resulting conflict on the shop floor play a key part in CallCentral. Like factory workers, call center agents may have to compromise the quality of the product ("the script" and answers to the script's questions) in order to meet their targets. Team leaders and campaign managers are aware of what upstairs would label agents' "subversive" practices, yet encourage those very practices. Equally, from time to time downstairs' subversion may become evident to upstairs. The reaction from above intends to halt the resistant practices for a moment. However, in trying to force the call center practices into a dualism of control and resistance, objections arise. First, actions from downstairs in the call center are collective, whereas in Burawoy's case the behaviors at issue are always individualistic and ineffective (the management always wins the fight). In addition, there is little evidence that script changes are disruptive. In fact, drawing on the points made in the conclusions of Chapters 3, 4, and 5 I argue that for several reasons, the notion of resistance does not fully explain the oral and hand-written changes to the script that occur in the journey from upstairs to downstairs and finally on the phone.

First, the upstairs-downstairs relationship is more about cooperation than about resistance. To achieve campaign goals of identifying leads, downstairs modifies the stipulations in the formal contract between the company and the client. The results are honed performances of a scripted skeleton. The secrecy around script changes downstairs is part of this relationship, and script changes are not deemed "disruptive" unless explicitly exposed. Campaign managers may express conscious ambivalence toward script changing practices, but they know what upstairs (and the client) want to hear and see from downstairs and they deliver that. This requires keeping upstairs content by telling them that downstairs follows the script verbatim, and by meeting targets and deadlines. Keeping upstairs content allows for more liberty downstairs, a freedom that permits non-disruptive secondary adjustment activities while agents work the lines (cf. Field note entry 4.2) (unless operations managers are on the floor).

Second, campaign managers respect the script and the clients' wishes, and do not frame hand-written changes to the script as resistance. Their justification for the changes (Field note entry 4.2) is that the client and upstairs may not know what is best for them and the campaign. Whether creating options for personalization or opening the door to listening to interlocutors, script alterations are not heroic individual acts but are part of the system regulated by campaign managers. Campaign managers' and team leaders' motivations are more like pragmatic instrumentalism, part of a "getting on" strategy.

Third, in a similar vein it could be argued that using the script and the eight-section framework for monitoring are desperate attempts by downstairs to maintain upstairs' expectations and to "get on" with the outbound call center work, which is characterized by the sheer diversity of languages entailed and its transient nature (cf. Chapter 2).

So if script changes are not resistance, how should they be characterized? A "getting on" strategy of instrumental pragmatism is perhaps the best option. There are other forms of agency in the call centers that might be best captured under other rubrics. One such example is Goffman's "secondary adjustment." Every participant group, not just the campaign managers, is aware of and accepts the primary adjustment of meeting the targets set by upstairs. In Chapters 4 and 5 there are several examples of implicit semi-authorized "secondary adjustments" to targets rather than scripts.

The voicemail strategy advocated by team leaders may be a good example of this. Agents use this strategy to meet unrealistic dial rates and still generate some viable and successful calls. Agents may spend mornings on substantive calls (when it is easier to get hold of people and to actually make a lead), and afternoons on dialing only numbers they know are voicemails to get their dial rates up. CallCentral mid-level managers know about this practice but do not object to it as it helps the company and the agents. This example of secondary adjustment is another form of "creative compliance" in the call center. In both the script-based cases of "getting on" and the target adjustments, campaign managers believe the practices are in the best interest of the company and the client, and in line with their professional ethics. Rather than displaying resistance, team leaders and agents work hard to help the call center achieve its goals through creative compliance.

So agents' convictions are somewhat justified: that their oral and handwritten alterations of a script are permissible, that their translations are appropriate reproductions in a different language and for a different cultural setting, and that they are doing their job properly when they retextualize a script. None of my informants mentioned that there could possibly be a problem with them changing a script, and they happily explain in detail how they do so, thus obviating any sense in which these activities might be resistance.

The ethos of pride agents express in owning their scripts belies notions of "resistance." Agents are not uncritical of their working conditions, but it is unrealistic dial rate targets for performance that they resist. Agents' priorities are lower targets to enable full implementation of a script's referential content on the phone, and to facilitate complete data entry. They believe rearranging priorities such as adjusting dial rate targets would promote successful calling and reliable database maintenance while supporting a sufficient quantity of numbers dialed. The leads clients and managers want are generated not by the immediate contact of a call, but with a connection made by a quality exchange.

The achilles heel of monitoring

The control dimension of the monitoring apparatus, which is stressed to such a degree in previous Foucauldian-inspired call center analyses in the literature, is a sign of "powerful" management (cf. e.g., Fernie and Metcalf 1998; Taylor and Bain 1999). However, at CallCentral, monitoring is rather ineffective. There are two explanations for this. One is that monitoring, especially listening in silently, is labor intensive, a fact that is acknowledged by only a few studies such as Lankshear et al. (2001). There are often more than 60 agents calling with three permanent team leaders who still have to work the lines, too. Even if the company did undertake full-time call monitoring, it would not be possible to monitor everyone simultaneously. The other explanation is that even if upstairs managers wanted to monitor agents downstairs to enforce verbatim recitation of a script, this would not be possible given the variety of languages spoken in the call center, let alone with the lack of manpower, resources, and funds.

The call center management already struggles with recruiting L1 (first language) speakers for campaigns. They often resort to language speakers who are not always fluent but only have intermediate or beginner's knowledge of a desired language. The accuracy of translation is not monitored by senior staff because seldom do they speak those languages. In fact, it is impossible to find anyone who can monitor all the languages in which calls are placed. To assign such an individual only for monitoring purposes would be a waste of their potential for the company. Agents at CallCentral, who often did not know the extent of the monitoring, did not describe the experience of electronic monitoring and surveillance as tight. Equally, Fernie and Metcalf's widely cited assertion that "the tyranny of the assembly line is but a Sunday school picnic compared with the control that management can exercise in computer telephony" (1998, 2) does not hold true for CallCentral. One could even argue that taking a Foucauldian perspective with its focus on control and resistance is misguided and prejudges the workplace. My observations suggest that there is in fact little to incite agents' resistance in the first place.

Upskilling

In the literature, it is reported that agents are forced to continuously recite a script in a smiley tone of voice, and are monitored to ensure compliance. For instance Mirchandani claims that "call center workers (…) experience scripts as de-skilling, repetitive, and tedious" (2004, 361). Cameron also blames them for turning a call center into a "deskilling and disempowering workplace" (2000, 124). Also along these lines, scripts are said to turn workers into robots, oppressing them by reducing their opportunity to develop the capacity to make decisions on their own or solve problems (cf. e.g., Korczynski 2002; Ritzer 2000).

In the case of CallCentral, the script is a productive workplace tool, not an instrument of oppressive subordination. There are grounds for agreeing with Leidner that "there are circumstances in which routines, even imposed routines, can be useful to workers" (Leidner 1993, 5; see also Cook-Gumperz 2001, 123). My ethnography illustrates the value of a script for agents at CallCentral. Rather than deskilling, the activities of personalizing a script, polishing it to achieve politeness, and generating a delivery that allows consultation require specialized textual and communicative skills that are recognized in promotions and mature in employees over time (Ritzer 1998; Stanworth 2000; Belt et al. 2002). Refashioning a script is an expert process (cf. also Woydack and Rampton 2016).

The majority of agents describe scripts as helpful, beneficial, and even upskilling for several reasons. For instance, it is often thanks to the script that people can to work in an IT call center despite having no prior technical knowledge or fluency in another language. Consequently, the call center often constitutes a stepping-stone for agents as it is often their first job in London and they can gain valuable work experience for other more prestigious jobs. In addition, scripts provide the structure for creative transformations that allow callers to connect with their interlocutors. Neither agents nor team leaders complained about scripts but instead worked to enhance them to interest potential customers.

Agents suggest that scripts help boost their confidence. Based on their accounts, agents enjoy personalizing scripts and changing them. It has become evident how much crafting, knowledge, and skill continuously goes into reworking the script on paper, improvising around it, and tailoring it to individual people on the other end of the phone. Agents usually begin their employment as callers by participating in script-based engagement campaigns that only allow minimal personalization of the script. Only once they have mastered this can they be trained in the more demanding consultative calling for BANT and nurturing campaigns. Thus an agent's progress in working with a script is officially recognized when mid-level managers move callers to high-end campaigns as their skills mature, and when higher management reflects its appreciation for leads in bonus payments. In general, agents' abilities to personalize scripts on paper and phone and to do consultative calling are examples of skills easily overlooked by an outsider; often they are summed up in the generic and indiscriminate term *communication skills* or equated with personality or gender.

Other researchers such as Belt et al. (2000, 2002), Muller (1999), and Houlihan (2003) also dispute the claim that call center work is unskilled or semi-skilled despite agents performing a narrow range of tasks in a standardized environment. They point out that there is often a joint desire among agents, supervisors, and call center managers to fight the mythologization of call center work as being unskilled, simple, and routine (Belt et al. 2000, 374). In a similar vein, Muller (1999, 31) claims that a substantial amount of the "knowledge work" carried out by these operatives is devalued and goes unrecognized because it is "invisible" to managers (and by extension to the larger public, including researchers) owing to their misguided assumptions about what agents' work involves (cf. McPhail 2002, 33). As a result, according to Belt et al. (2000, 381), even the so-called communication skills so sought after in the call center industry are not valued adequately outside this context and are often degraded.

Having now discussed the practical findings and implications of this study I now look closely at the intertwining of standardization and transformation.

The essential intertwining of standardization and transformation

On an abstract level, there have been several attempts to theorize contrasts between standardization in theory and in practice in organizations beyond call centers. The most applicable to the context here is Brunsson and Jacobssen's theorization (2000). The authors argued that weak organizations have to rely on standardization as a soft form of regulation. Specifically, for the standard to be "implemented" or practiced, it has to be "transformed" first. This transformation involves two aspects: (i) "from talk to action—what the standard says is translated into what the follower does," and (ii) "from the general to the specific—the general requirement of the standard is translated into the follower's own specific practice" (2000: 128). Schools, for example, often have to follow a standard of self-evaluations in which parents and students fill out self-evaluation forms. But this is not enough, for schools also have to show other parties that they act on this standardization. They are likely to initiate new projects, "citing them as examples of evaluation to parties such as politicians, parents, and audit offices" (Brunsson and Jacobsson 2000, 3). In this case, they suggest "standardization involves the translation from action to talk, from specific to the general, from own activity to categories that can be understood by others."

Brunsson and Jacobssen (2000, 130) further cite extensive research on individuals and organizations (e.g., Brunsson 1995) that indicates there may be significant "differences between presentation and practice, between formal structures and actual operations, and between what people say and what they do (…)." They explain this on the basis that actors possess dual systems detached from one another; consequently, actors may claim that they abide by a standard, although in practice they do not. Standardizers rarely appear to note this phenomenon, or at least rarely discuss and acknowledge it in public. Conversely, Brunsson and Jacobssen conclude standardizers appear to suppose "that standards, that change presentation, always change practice" (2000, 130).

If we apply this theorem to CallCentral, it is notable that downstairs has to show that they comply with the script. In this case, this is done through monitoring, call outcomes, and ultimately through the various forms of statistics. These practices are understandable to outsiders, such as the client and upstairs, shareholders, or even scholars, and they demonstrate compliance. Nonetheless, there is clearly a mismatch between presentation and practices, encompassing a range from monitoring to reading the script verbatim to translation and personalization. We have seen that there may be pragmatic reasons why the presentation upstairs to the client contradicts the practice on the call center floor. In the end, it is both in upstairs' and downstairs' interest that the concept of agents reading the standardized script on the phone is maintained. Without this presentation of textual fidelity and of strict monitoring control (including the accurate production of statistics and meeting of targets) to outsiders, upstairs would probably be less able to attract clients and there would be less work for downstairs (cf. Chapter 3; Smith 1996, 181–182).

Viterna and Manyard (2002, 367) suggest that with standardization today being prized across the world, it is difficult for businesses and organizations to ignore it. However, they point out that, regarding the history of survey interview research, it was only from the 1950s that standardization of wording was introduced. Previously, interviewers were "expected to standardize the meaning of the question," but "were given freedom to modify" the wording of the question (Viterna and Maynard 2002, 366). They found in their study that there was a remarkable contrast between standardization (standardization in theory) and what agents were trained and permitted to do (standardization in practice). So, to go back to CallCentral, from downstairs' perspective the standardization of a script is in terms of meaning. Agents change wording in the service of connecting with interlocutors and highlighting important elements in the script.

Moving beyond standardization and stigma in the study of call centers

This book does not suggest that CallCentral was an easy place to work, and although scripts were not the main source of stress, agents mentioned struggling with monotony, repetition, and unrealistic targets. In this account, I offered some examples of agents' attempts to meet their targets using a trick, the voicemail strategy. They do this so they can follow a script (guaranteeing the quality of a call) and still achieve unrealistic targets for the quantity of calls they must make. Thus unrealistic targets, more than scripts, are the main stressor. This is in line with previous studies on workplace standardization, especially research on factories such as that by Burawoy (1979). Ironically, what is praised in many management textbooks today as a motivational tool to improve productivity—in this case, unrealistically high targets—seems to have the opposite effect, particularly in relation to quality at CallCentral. Team leaders and managers were aware that unrealistic targets have the opposite effect from the one desired. Even upstairs seems to have understood this when they tried to steer the call center away from engagement campaigns and increasingly toward nurturing campaigns that allow more quality time on the phone. Nurturing campaigns do not have targets as such and there is less stress on quantity. In addition, the contracts tend to endure for longer periods of time, meaning that agents are paid more and have longer guaranteed employment.

However, it has become evident that despite the script and monitoring, workers do not believe their talk is homogenized or that they lose their agency in their tasks. Although some do mention their struggle with monotony and the fight against repetition (Chapter 5), they overcome this by personalizing and varying their script. In this respect, my findings are similar to what has been observed in anthropological and sociological ethnographic studies of factories. For instance, Timmermans and Epstein (2010, 83) claim that workers successfully resisted the Taylorization of the assembly line and the Fordist production regime. In a similar vein, Edgell points out the "widespread agreement that the dominance of Fordism, especially in the most advanced industrial capitalist societies, has come to end, and with it the security of standard work (…)" (Edgell 2006, 100). It has been replaced by neo-Fordism or post- Fordism or more specifically, new production lines such as those of *Toyota* or *Volvo*, by de-standardization and team work. These have been shown to be more successful than Taylorization, inciting less resistance from workers, less absenteeism, and higher work satisfaction and productivity (cf. Watson 2008, 114; Edgell 2006, 85–87).

The question of why supposedly failed Taylorist and Fordist practices are now being introduced into the public sector is an interesting one. This issue has been discussed in other fields, for example, under the term "audit cultures" or "audit society" (Shore and Wright 2015; Strathern 2000; Power 2010). The more relevant question concerns why "standardization" in the call center is often framed in a discussion about the problematic side of scripts instead of discussion about targets. In other words, why is there such concern over the use of scripts as forms of standardization producing the negative assessments of call centers?

I have suggested that there are three reasons for stigmatizing call center labor: (i) the history of standardization in social theory, (ii) the epistemological framework typically used in call center research, and (iii) the methods used by researchers. By taking the view that standardization is not necessarily negative and that call centers are not inherently problematic, it has emerged that there are some positive aspects to call center labor and scripts, and that working as call center agents might actually promote the developing skills of some people. For instance, Cook-Gumperz (2001) suggests based on Leidner's (1993) study that "a scripted environment provides an ideal site to bring together a culturally diverse workforce" and that "the scripted communicative work environment makes a good learning context for interactional exchange" (2001, 125). My study supports these conclusions (see also Woydack 2016).

Although findings here are based on the data from one call center, many of my informants have worked in other call centers and at other jobs, allowing their evaluations of call center work to be generalized more widely. For instance, a few interviewees compared their call center experience to the retail sector and reported, in contrast to the commonly held view in the literature (e.g., Cameron 2000; Bain and Taylor 2000), that call centers are "much more relaxed." These same informants lamented the gulf between the reality of call centers and the representations and stigmatization of them in the media.

My purpose is not to extricate call center working conditions from debate, even though I have contested the demonization of calling scripts in particular (cf. Woydack and Rampton 2016). I intend to challenge the stigmatization of call centers as twenty-first century sweatshops (Hudson 2011). The stigmatizing that occurs in the literature is not only simplistic but constitutes the devaluation of many people's working lives. In interviews, agents reported experiencing stigma for working in a call center and tried to hide their employment in conversations with outsiders (Woydack 2017).

Making explicit the skills these employees recognize and master as part of their jobs would require more introspection than most can mobilize. Political arguments have tended to dominate call center and standardization discourses. These entail large- scale generalizations and strategic essentialism in the service of critiquing oppression. Valuable as this may be for some purposes, as Woydack and Rampton (2016, 729) write, "in our work on race and ethnicity, we do hold that in the process of abstracting and simplifying, it is vital to refer back continuously to what is "lived" in the everyday, and that, ultimately, both academic and political generalizations should be made accountable to the sorts of ground-level understanding attempted [in this book] (…) (Harris and Rampton 2010; Hymes 1964)."

My stance, while unusual, is not unique. Eminent Foucauldian sociologist Nicolas Rose, for example, argues that "the notion of resistance, at least as it has conventionally functioned, (…) is too simple and flattening… [Instead,] one [s]hould examine the [much smaller] ways in which creativity arises out of the situation of human beings engaged in particular relations of force and meaning, and what is made out of the possibilities of that location" (1999, 279–280). Rose's position further supports the suggestion that "resistance" is indeed not a helpful construct when discussing scripting in call centers (cf. Woydack and Rampton 2016).

To conclude, this book does not aim to provide a verdict on call centers, a diverse array of complex organizations in countries around the world. A verdict would not even be possible with a single case study. Equally, it does not aim to suggest alternative proposals to script-centered working practices. Instead, this linguistic ethnography of a calling script has provided a detailed, complex, and lived account of the situated details of communicative practice, beyond interdisciplinary, ideological, and historical debates that have too rigidly characterized call centers through their scripted and standardized practices.

References

Ackroyd, Stephen, and Paul Thompson. 1999. *Organizational Misbehaviour*. London/Thousand Oaks: Sage.

Bain, Peter, and Phil Taylor. 2000. Entrapped by the 'Electronic Panopticon'? Worker Resistance in the Call Centre. *New Technology, Work and Employment* 15 (1): 2–18.

Belt, Vicki, Ranald Richardson, and Juliet Webster. 2000. Women's Work in the Information Economy: The Case of Telephone Call Centres. *Information, Communication & Society* 3 (3): 366–385.

———. 2002. Women, Social Skill and Interactive Service Work in Telephone Call Centres. *New Technology, Work and Employment* 17 (1): 20–34.

Brunsson, Nils. 1995. Ideas and Actions: Justification and Hypocrisy as Alternatives to Control. *Sociology of Organizations* 13: 211–235.

Brunsson, Nils, and Bengt Jacobsson. 2000. *A World of Standards*. Oxford/New York: Oxford University Press.

Burawoy, Michael. 1979. *Manufacturing Consent: Changes in the Labor Process under Monopoly Capitalism*. Chicago: University of Chicago Press.

Cameron, Deborah. 2000. *Good to Talk?* London: Sage.

Cook-Gumperz, Jenny. 2001. Cooperation, Collaboration and Pleasure in Work. Culture in Communication: Analyses of Intercultural Situations. In *Culture in Communication: Analyses of Intercultural Situations*, ed. Aldo Di Luzio, Susanne Günthner, and Franca Orletti, 117–139. Amsterdam: John Benjamins Publishing.

Edgell, Steven. 2006. *The Sociology of Work: Continuity and Change in Paid and Unpaid Work*. London: Sage.

Fernie, Sue, and David Metcalf. 1998. *(Not) Hanging on the Telephone: Payment Systems in the New Sweatshops*. London: London School of Economics, Centre for Economic Performance.

Goffman, Erving. 1961. *Asylums: Essays on the Social Situation of Mental Patients and Other Institutions*. London: Penguin Books.

Harris, Roxy, and Ben Rampton. 2010. Ethnicities Without Guarantees: An Empirical Approach. In *Identity in the 21st Century: New Trends in Changing Times*, ed. Magaret Wetherell, 95–119. Basingstoke: Palgrave Macmillan.

Holman, David, and Sue Fernie. 2000. Can I Help You? Call Centres and Job Satisfaction. *Centrepiece Magazine* 5 (1). http://cep.lse.ac.uk/centrepiece/v05i1/holman_fernie.pdf

Houlihan, Maeve. 2003. Making Sense of Call Centres: Working and Managing the Front Line. Unpublished, University of Lancaster, Lancaster.

Hudson, Alex. 2011. Are Call Centres the Factories of the 21st Century. *BBC News*.

Hymes, Dell. 1964. Introduction: Toward Ethnographies of Communication1. *American Anthropologist* 66 (6_PART2): 1–34.

Keesing, Roger M. 1981. *Cultural Anthropology: A Contemporary Perspective*. 2d ed. New York: Holt, Rinehart, and Winston.

Korczynski, Marek. 2002. *Human Resource Management in Service Work*, Management, Work and Organisations. Basingstoke: Palgrave Macmillan.

Lankshear, Gloria, Peter Cook, David Mason, Sally Coates, and Graham Button. 2001. Call Centre Employees' Responses to Electronic Monitoring: Some Research Findings. *Work, Employment and Society* 15 (3): 595–605.

Leidner, Robin. 1993. *Fast Food, Fast Talk: Service Work and the Routinization of Everyday Life*. Berkeley: University of California Press.

Linstead, Steve. 1985. Jokers Wild: The Importance of Humour in the Maintenance of Organizational Culture. *The Sociological Review* 33 (4): 741–767.

Marchington, M. 1992. Managing Labour Relations in a Competitive Environment. In *Skill and Consent: Contemporary Studies in the Labour Process*, ed. Andrew Sturdy, David Knights, and Hugh Willmott, 149–185. London: Routledge.

McPhail, Brenda. 2002. *What Is 'on the Line' in Call Centre Studies? A Review of Key Issues on Academic Literature*. University of Toronto. http://www3.fis.utoronto.ca/research/iprp/publications/mcphail-cc.pdf.

Mirchandani, Kiran. 2004. Practices of Global Capital: Gaps, Cracks and Ironies in Transnational Call Centres in India. *Global Networks* 4 (4): 355–373.

Muller, Michael J. 1999. Invisible Work of Telephone Operators: An Ethnocritical Analysis. *Computer Supported Cooperative Work (CSCW)* 8 (1–2): 31–61.

Mumby, Dennis K. 2005. Theorizing Resistance in Organization Studies: A Dialectical Approach. *Management Communication Quarterly* 19 (1): 19–44.

O'Reilly, Karen. 2009. *Key Concepts in Ethnography*, Sage Key Concepts. Los Angeles: Sage.

Power, Michael. 2010. *The Audit Society: Rituals of Verification*. Reprinted. Oxford: Oxford University Press.

Ritzer, George. 1998. *The McDonaldization Thesis: Explorations and Extensions*. London/Thousand Oaks: Sage.

———. 2000. *The McDonaldization of Society*. New Century ed. Thousand Oaks: Pine Forge Press.

Rose, Nikolas. 1999. *Powers of Freedom: Reframing Political Thought*. Cambridge: Cambridge University Press.

Roy, Donald. 1959. 'Banana Time': Job Satisfaction and Informal Interaction. *Human Organization* 18 (4): 158–168.

Shire, Karen, Ursula Holtgrewe, and Christian Kerst. 2002. Re-Organising Service Work: Call Centres in Germany and Britain: An Introduction. In *Re-Organising Service Work: Call Centres in Germany and Britain*, ed. Ursula Holtgrewe, Christian Kerst, and Karen Shire, 1–19. Aldershot/Hants/Burlington: Ashgate.

Shore, Cris, and Susan Wright. 2015. Governing by Numbers: Audit Culture, Rankings and the New World Order: Governing by Numbers. *Social Anthropology* 23 (1): 22–28.

Smith, Dorothy E. 1996. The Relations of Ruling: A Feminist Inquiry. *Studies in Cultures, Organizations and Societies* 2 (2): 171–190.

Stanworth, Celia. 2000. Women and Work in the Information Age. *Gender, Work and Organization* 7 (1): 20–32.

Strathern, Marilyn, ed. 2000. *Audit Cultures: Anthropological Studies in Accountability, Ethics, and the Academy*, European Association of Social Anthropologists. London/New York: Routledge.

Taylor, Steve. 1998. Emotional Labour and the New Workplace. In *Workplaces of the Future*, ed. Paul Thompson and Chris Warhurst, 84–103. London: Macmillan Education UK.

Taylor, Phil, and Peter Bain. 1999. An Assembly Line in the Head': Work and Employee Relations in the Call Centre. *Industrial Relations Journal* 30 (2): 101–117.

Timmermans, Stefan, and Steven Epstein. 2010. A World of Standards but Not a Standard World: Toward a Sociology of Standards and Standardization. *Annual Review of Sociology* 36 (1): 69–89.

Viterna, Jocelyn, and Douglas Maynard. 2002. How Uniform Is Standardization? Variation Within and Across Survey Research Centre Reading Protocols for Interviewing. In *Standardization and Tacit Knowledge-Interaction and Practice in the Survey Interview*, ed. Douglas Maynard, Hanneke Houtkoop-Steenstra, Nora Schaeffer, and Johannes van der Zouwen, 365–401. New York: Wiley.

Warde, Alan. 1992. Industrial Discipline: Factory Regime and Politics in Lancaster. In *Skill and Consent: Contemporary Studies in the Labour Process*, ed. Andrew Sturdy, David Knights, and Hugh Willmott, 97–114. London: Routledge.

Watson, Tony J. 2008. *Sociology, Work and Industry*. 5th ed. London /New York: Routledge.

Woydack, Johanna. 2016. Superdiversity and a London Multilingual Call Centre. In *Engaging Superdiversity: Recombining Spaces, Times and Language Practices*, ed. Karel Arnaut, Martha Sif Karrebaek, Massimiliano Spotti, and Jan Blommaert, vol. 7, 220–251. Bristol: Multilingual Matters.

———. 2017. *Call Center Agents and the Experience of Stigma*. Working Papers in Urban Language Literacies. King's College London. https://www.academia.edu/33711030/WP215_Woydack_2017._Call_center_agents_and_the_experience_of_stigma

Woydack, Johanna, and Ben Rampton. 2016. Text Trajectories in a Multilingual Call Centre: The Linguistic Ethnography of a Calling Script. *Language in Society* 45 (05): 709–732.

Appendix 1: Glossary of Terms

Asset:	An offering from a company intended to be shared with the recipients of agents' calls. Another term for collateral. A selection of media, e.g., reports or e-books, used to support sales or services. These assets can serve as bait.
BANT (Budget, Authority, Need, Timeframe) campaigns:	Campaigns in which agents ask several (profiling) questions of those they target in their calls regarding a potential project (including Budget, Authority, Need, Timeframe). These campaigns are more expensive and technical than the Engagement campaigns, but not as technical as Nurturing campaigns.
Call to Action:	In marketing, the concept of prompting people to do something (e.g., click on something) through the use of texts and graphics (e.g., an email or script).

© The Author(s) 2019
J. Woydack, *Linguistic Ethnography of a Multilingual Call Center:
London Calling*, Communicating in Professions and Organizations,
https://doi.org/10.1007/978-3-319-93323-8

Call Outcome: The result of the call an agent makes. The possible outcomes are first predicted by the campaign manager, categorized, and agents are then required to log a result or outcome for each call. The logging of call outcomes is necessary to generate statistics such as the dial report.

Collateral: A selection of media, e.g., reports or e-books, used to support sales or services. Collaterals are also known as assets.

Campaign Managers: The management of the call center in charge of managing campaigns.

Closing Statement: Agents are required by law to close a successful call by stating that the client will call back the person contacted over the phone.

Convergence Rates: A range of formulas used to calculate the success of the composition of a script based on the statistics generated by agents' calls and the actions of those receiving calls (opened the email told about, opened the attachment).

Dial Report: The statistics that detail how long individual agents spent on the phone and the call outcome they logged after the call.

Dial Sheet: A summary of the number of dials and leads all agents on all campaigns have made. The summary can be refreshed and updated every minute (online) and is accessible from upstairs and downstairs.

Engagement Campaign: The goal is to convince potential customers to engage with the client via email or phone. The cheapest and least technical campaigns. They have no profiling questions on the pitch, the main part of the script.

Nurturing Campaign:	These are the most expensive and technical of all campaigns run in the call center. There are usually many long and detailed questions on a script that may be five pages long. The goal is to nurture "leads" till they are ready to buy.
Lead:	A contact that agrees to all the questions on the script and his/her company matches the campaign criteria for the lead definition. They must also agree to speak to the client after the initial call.
Master Script:	The final script approved by the client.
Operations Manager:	The call center's big boss from upstairs.
Pitch:	The most important part of the script. It is campaign specific and will have been approved by the client. The goal is to convey the specific message that the clients want potential customers to hear.
Sales Brief:	A written summary of a client's needs and wishes. It gives a preliminary view of the type of leads desired, lead criteria, and the collaterals. The sales brief will then become the agents' brief.
Whitepaper:	A collateral report that is emailed to the contact.

Appendix 2: Transcription Conventions

[ ]	Inaudible word
(…)	Text omitted
[text]	Words that are necessary for the text to make sense or any other additions
(word)	Word that I believe the interviewee said based on the transcription
((laugh))	Description of what the informant did
(sic)	Grammatical error produced by the interviewees which I did not correct

© The Author(s) 2019

209

J. Woydack, *Linguistic Ethnography of a Multilingual Call Center:*
London Calling, Communicating in Professions and Organizations,
https://doi.org/10.1007/978-3-319-93323-8

Index

© The Author(s) 2019   **211**
J. Woydack, *Linguistic Ethnography of a Multilingual Call Center:*
London Calling, Communicating in Professions and Organizations,
https://doi.org/10.1007/978-3-319-93323-8

Printed by Printforce, the Netherlands